Jealous Gods and Chosen People

Jealous Gods and Chosen People

The Mythology of the Middle East

David Leeming

OXFORD
UNIVERSITY PRESS

OXFORD
UNIVERSITY PRESS

Oxford University Press, Inc., publishes works that further
Oxford University's objective of excellence
in research, scholarship, and education.

Oxford   New York
Auckland   Cape Town   Dar es Salaam   Hong Kong   Karachi
Kuala Lumpur   Madrid   Melbourne   Mexico City   Nairobi
New Delhi   Shanghai   Taipei   Toronto

With offices in
Argentina   Austria   Brazil   Chile   Czech Republic   France   Greece
Guatemala   Hungary   Italy   Japan   Poland   Portugal   Singapore
South Korea   Switzerland   Thailand   Turkey   Ukraine   Vietnam

First published by Oxford University Press, Inc., 2004
198 Madison Avenue, New York, New York 10016
www.oup.com

First issued as an Oxford University Press paperback, 2005
ISBN-13: 978-019-518252-1
ISBN-10: 0-19-518252-9

Oxford is a registered trademark of Oxford University Press

The library of Congress has cataloged the cloth edition as follows:
Leeming, David Adams, 1937–
Jealous gods and chosen people : the mythology of the middle east /
David Leeming.
p. cm. — Includes bibliographical references and index.
ISBN-13: 978-019-514789-6
ISBN-10: 0-19-514789-8
1. Mythology, Middle Eastern.   I. Title.
BL1060.L43 2004   291.1'3'09394—dc21   2003053596

Drawings on pages 33, 34, 35, 36 by Jake Page.

1 3 5 7 9 8 6 4 2

Printed in the United States of America

Contents

Preface

The purpose of this book is to provide a comprehensive study of the mythologies of the area of the world that has been called, with varying degrees of inclusion and/or accuracy, the Middle East, the Near East, the Levant, and the Fertile Crescent. In colonial British usage the "Near East" was the Balkans and Asia Minor. More recently it has been used more or less interchangeably with the "Middle East." The Fertile Crescent is the fertile land forming an arch around the Syrian steppes and including the eastern Mediterranean coastal lands beginning with Egypt in the west, southeastern Anatolia (Asian Turkey) in the north, and Mesopotamia ("between the rivers," referring to the Tigris and Euphrates—present-day Iraq) in the east. "Levant" was a term used primarily by the Europeans in reference to the countries bordering the eastern Mediterranean. The term comes from the old French word meaning "rising," referring to the rising of the sun in the east or Orient. In common usage, particularly in the geopolitical context, the term "Middle East" has assimilated all of the above designations, referring to the areas of Asia and Africa bordered by Libya in the west and Pakistan in the east, and including Turkey in the north and the Arabian Peninsula in the south. In this book, then, "Middle East" includes all of the land masses to which the various terms in question refer.

Because myths of various cultures both reflect and affect history and because the mythology and religion of one culture can directly influence the mythology and religion of others, I have divided the book into two parts, the first containing historical background, the second containing the myths themselves. In Part One, rather than treating the histories of the given cultures and nations in isolation, I have attempted to give a sense of the interactions of all of the various groups in the region during given time periods. In Part Two, selected myths of the Middle East are retold against the background of Part One, that is, in the context of history, geography, language, and religion.

The ancient cultures covered here include those of Egypt, Mesopotamia (the Sumerians, Elamites, and Kassites, the Semitic Akkadians, Amorites, Babylonians, Mesopotamian Hurrians, and Assyrians), the Anatolian Hurrians and Hittites, and the Western Semitic peoples living in lands known at various times as a whole or in part as Canaan, Palestine, Phoenicia, Aram, Israel, Judah, and Samaria, with the addition of Arabia. Also considered will be the stories of Christianity and Islam, the two modern religions that, with Judaism, have their sources in the area in question. The mythology of pre-Islamic Iran is not fully included here, as it seems more in tune with the religious traditions of Vedic India than with those of the Middle East.

Given the particular importance of the region to political, economic, and religious questions of the present day, the mythologies of the ancient people of the Middle East will sometimes suggest comparisons with current situations. The events and stories under consideration here cannot be reasonably separated from the recent history of the part of the world that includes modern-day Iraq, Turkey, Egypt, Syria, Lebanon, Israel, Palestine, Jordan, Yemen, the Gulf states, and Saudi Arabia. The Middle East today is a battleground for the struggle between major nationalized religious traditions, particularly Israeli Jew and Arab Muslim (with significant Western Christian participation). The sources of this struggle can be traced in part to ancient antagonisms in the region, particularly between closely related Semites, and specifically to mythologies that have evolved there in various religious and national contexts since prehistory.

As always when discussing mythology, it is important to define terms. The myths collected and discussed here are for the most part *religious* narratives that transcend the possibilities of common experience and that express any given culture's literal or metaphorical understanding of various aspects of reality. In this sense myths have to do with the relation of the culture, or of human beings in general, to the unknown in the cosmos. To so-called fundamentalists of any given culture the religious stories of that culture are literally true, while stories of other cultures and religions are understood to be mere folklore—what in common usage we in fact mean by "myth." For others, both within given cultures and outside of them, myths are seen as important metaphorical constructs reflecting understandings that cannot be expressed in any other way. For many mythologists these literally false stories are "true" in the sense that they form an actual, real part of any culture's identity. What are Hopis without the kachina myths, the ancient Norse people without Odin, the Greeks without the deeds of Apollo, Dionysos, and Odysseus, the Jews without Yahweh's covenant, the Christians without the resurrection? Understood in this way, it is possible to speak of the "myths" of the three monotheistic Abrahamic religions just as we speak of the "myths" of the ancient peoples whose sacred stories are no longer treated as the scripture of viable religions. The Hebrew story of the parting of the Sea of Reeds or the Christian story of the resurrection of Jesus are myths to Hindus, as is the Zuni creation story to Christians or the concept of Brahman to Jews. But with nonexclusionary vision, other people's religious narratives can be seen as tribe-defining cultural dreams and as significant metaphors that can speak truthfully to people across cultural and sectarian boundaries.

Part One

THE HISTORICAL BACKGROUND

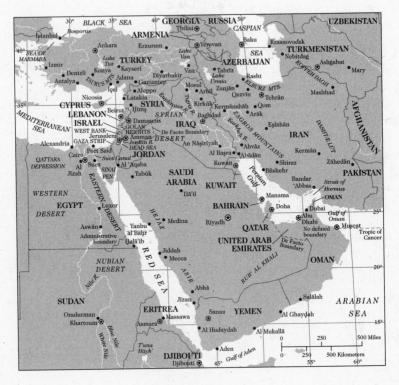

The Middle East Today

1

Prehistory

The Paleolithic Age

As is the case with other parts of the world, the emergence of the human species in the Middle East is difficult to establish. There are archeological indications—primarily rough stone tools and skeletal remains—of the presence of an early hominid species (*Homo erectus*) in the area dating from at least 300,000 B.C.E., the period known as the lower (early) Paleolithic (Old Stone Age, c. 2 million–100,000 B.C.E.—geologically the Ice Age or the Pleistocene). These people would have been nomadic hunter-gatherers. Crude stone carvings indicate a possible mythological or religious consciousness. But it is not until the Middle Paleolithic (c. 100,000–30,000 B.C.E.) that we find Middle Eastern evidence of a hominid species—in this case so-called Neanderthal man—who was clearly moving in the direction of the kind of activity that would characterize later humans. In the archeological site of Shanidar in Iraq, for instance, graves contain bodies that appear to have been positioned ritualistically, indicating, at the very least, a sense of community responsibility that stands in opposition to the popular image of the "caveman." Neanderthal man remained, however, like his predecessor, a hunter-gatherer, of whom we know relatively little, and in any case by about 30,000 B.C.E. Neanderthals had been displaced in the area by our own hominid subspecies, *Homo sapiens*, who first arrived in the Middle East perhaps as

early as 90,000 B.C.E. During the Upper or Late Paleolithic
(c. 30,000–10,000 B.C.E.), these humans made significant strides
toward the civilizations that would develop in future millennia. Excavations such as those at Kom Ombo and Jebel Sahaba in Egypt reveal
a relatively sophisticated tool and weapon industry and clearly ritualistic burial practices. The rapid expansion of the Sahara, perhaps associated with the long drought brought about by a cold spell
1,000–1,300 years long (the so-called Younger Dryas, about 12,000
years ago), seems to have forced people to remain for long periods
near the Nile River, thus causing the building of more or less permanent settlements. The drought in question affected the entire region
of the eastern Mediterranean, in fact, and made necessary certain
changes in the old hunter-gatherer cultures. The emergence in the
Levant of agriculture and settlements and still more sophisticated
toolmaking mark a transitional period from the Paleolithic to the
Neolithic (New Stone Age) known as the Mesolithic (Middle Stone
Age) or Epipaleolithic or Proto-Neolithic (c. 10,000–8,000 B.C.E.,
depending upon the location). During this period hunting and gathering remained the dominant sources of food, but agricultural practices were gradually developed, as were the storage of food, the
beginning of the domestication of animals, and the building of more
complex permanent settlements that were, in effect, the precursors of
the truly permanent settlements of the great cultures that would
emerge in the Neolithic Age (c. 8000–3000 B.C.E.).

Natufian Culture

Central to the Mesolithic development in the Middle East was the
Natufian culture, so named after a site north of Jerusalem. Natufian
settlements for between 100 and 150 people were scattered throughout the Mesolithic Middle East. Among the best known of these are
Tell ("mound" in Arabic) Mureybet in the upper Euphrates Valley (in
modern Syria), Hayonim (in modern Israel), and Tell es-Sultan (near
Jericho in modern Palestine). An element of particular interest in the
Natufian culture is the apparent establishment of protosettlements
even before the period of the Younger Dryas—that is to say, before
the necessary advent of primitive agriculture. An example of such a
settlement is Tell Abu Hureyra, near Lake Assad in modern Syria,

which was populated from c. 10,500 B.C.E. and which appears not to
have cultivated grain until some 450 years later. Tell es-Sultan, a
Natufian site near Jericho, also seems to have been settled before the
development of agriculture. The urge to settle in one place may have
been the result of abundant wild food resources in the immediate
area. Tell Abu Hureyra and other Natufian settlements were abandoned late in the Mesolithic period, perhaps because of overutiliza-
tion of resources or intertribal violence. When Tell Abu Hureyra was
reestablished, it was one of the many examples of what has come to be
known as the "Neolithic Revolution."

The Neolithic Revolution

Revolution is perhaps not the best word to attach to a process that was
gradual rather than instantaneous. Still, the changes that occurred
during the period in question (8000–3000 B.C.E.) are comparable to
other periods of radical change such as the Industrial Revolution of
the nineteenth century or the current technological revolution. What
had happened in the Middle East by the end of the Neolithic was a
radical change from a life based on hunting and gathering to one centered primarily on agriculture, animal husbandry, and community living based on civil and religious law and ritual, with accompanying
mythology. Along with these changes came technological improve-
ments in weaponry and tools, the development of pottery to store
grains, and bricks to build houses.

The Neolithic period in the Middle East saw the domestication of
sheep in northern Mesopotamia by 8000 B.C.E. and the cultivation of
grains in Palestine and Anatolia during the eighth and seventh millennia B.C.E. Over the centuries the variety of grains and domesti-
cated animals grew, as did the size of settlements. There are
indications that cult centers developed at Jericho and in Mureybet
and Çayonu in the Euphrates Valley as well as in Hacilar and Çatal
Hüyük in Anatolia.

The Neolithic Cultures

One result of the Neolithic revolution was the establishment during
the fourth millennium B.C.E. of cities—as opposed to the family-clan

villages or towns of the Neolithic—beginning in southern Mesopotamia. This was an age in which not only did farming develop, but
much more sophisticated metal tools and weapons replaced imple-
ments of wood and stone. An insufficiency of rainfall necessitated a
strong government that could organize irrigation and other specialized activities involved in the highly interactive living of a relatively
large population. The integrative aspect of the early cities was accen-
tuated by surrounding walls meant to delineate boundaries and to
protect against invaders. And organized religions with temples, a
priestly caste, and highly developed mythologies provided further ra-
tionale for the existence of even larger city-states. In effect, these early
cities and city-states were the foundation for what would become the
religious or myth-based nationalism that is still so much a part of human life.

The Ubaids and Sumerians

The people who developed the first great cities were the people of
Kengir, now southern Iraq. Their later Semitic conquerors called their
land Sumer, and we know of them as the Sumerians. The Sumerians,
whose origins are a mystery, were unrelated to the Semites, who would
eventually conquer them. They probably arrived in Mesopotamia from
Central Asia in the fourth millennium B.C.E. (Wolkstein and Kramer,
116) and mixed with other non-Semitic people, called Ubaids, who
had been there from at least the fifth millennium B.C.E. The Ubaids
are so called for Tell Ubaid, near the ruins of the ancient city of Ur. It
was the Ubaid culture that first established protocities along the
marshland of what is now southern Iraq. These settlements included
what became the Sumerian cities of Ur, Eridu, Adab, Isin, Larsa, Lagash, Nippur, and Unug (better known by its later Semitic name,
Uruk or Erech). The Ubaids were skilled at farming, animal husbandry, pottery, and other crafts.

The period immediately following the Ubaid is generally called the
Early and Middle Uruk periods (c. 4000–3500 B.C.E.). By then nomadic Semitic tribes from the northwest and Arabia had mingled
with and gained considerable influence over Ubaid. Then came
Sumerian dominance in the so-called Protoliterate and Late Uruk

Sumerian periods, c. 3500–3100 B.C.E. These designations vary considerably among scholars, and there are some who suggest that the Sumerians were direct descendants of the Ubaids (Black and Green, 11; Jacobsen, "Mesopotamian Religions," 447). The Late Uruk period coincided with the predynastic period of Egypt and the proto-Elamite (Tall-i-Malyan) period in Persia (Iran).

Late Uruk or predynastic Sumer is characterized by elements that we associate with the word *civilization*. Elaborate sculpture, monumental architecture, and a governmental assembly with elected religious and civil leaders, headed by an equal among equals called the *ensi* (a system that can be contrasted with the federated government of overlords who ruled neighboring Elam until the rise of the Awan or Shustar dynasty there in c. 2700 B.C.E.), are some of these elements. But the most important contribution of the Sumerians of the late fourth millennium B.C.E. was writing.

The Ancient Middle East

2

The Bronze Age

The Invention of Writing

History can be said to begin when records are kept for later people to read. To the extent that this is so, prehistory ended and history began at Sumer. It is easy to imagine that the need grew for a means of keeping track of the complexities of irrigation, animal husbandry, planting schedules, trade, government, religious activities, and various religious stories, such as the creation myths and the "biographies" and deeds of the particular city gods that provided a given people with cultural identity and significance. The Sumerians had by about 3400 B.C.E. discovered the solution to the need to record these things by inventing a writing system that was a major step beyond the old clay pictographic token system that had long been used by many cultures for merely quantitative records. They established a script in which pictographs and later ideograms, or words that convey whole concepts, were augmented by phonemes, that is, symbols indicating differentiated sounds in the spoken Sumerian language. Cuneiform (from Latin *cuneus,* "wedge," and *forma,* "shape") is the name given to this writing system, which took the form of symbols pressed into little boxes on clay tablets. Not long after Sumerian writing, the Egyptians developed hieroglyphs, and a kind of proto-Elamite writing might have emerged in southern Persia. Certainly cuneiform had developed there by the third millennium B.C.E., as it had in Hittite Anatolia by the second millennium.

The Rise of Egypt

During the development of the Sumerian civilization, the great nation of Egypt was rising in the southwestern region of the Middle East. It was a land populated by people speaking an Afro-Asiatic language of the Hamitic branch, distantly related to the Semitic languages. Early Egyptians were nomadic, but during the predynastic period they formed communities, especially within the Badarian culture in the south, where agriculture had become particularly important. Also present by 4000 B.C.E. were advanced agricultural tools, decorated pottery, and figurines. By the end of the predynastic period Egyptians had built substantial boats, which they used for trade along the Nile and in other parts of the Middle East, including Sumer.

Important continuing developments during the period were the afterlife mythology and funeral architecture and practices that characterize ancient Egypt. By 3500 B.C.E. architectural models were buried with the dead to provide solace in the afterlife. During late predynastic times (the Gerzean or Naqada II period, c. 3400 B.C.E.) large, elaborately decorated and furnished tombs were built to house deceased people of status.

Early in the third millennium B.C.E. a united Egypt emerged as the first great nation-state. The unifier of the Egyptian state, marking the beginning of the Early Dynastic period, was either Narmer (c. 3110–3056 B.C.E.) or his son Aha; the two are known in combination as Menes. Traditionally it is Menes who founded the first capital at Memphis (near modern Cairo) and established his reign in association with the god Horus. By the end of the period, however, north and south had once again been separated, but by about 2800 B.C.E. the kingdom was reunited with a new religion centered on the god Atum, or Re, at Heliopolis (also near Cairo). So began the period known as the Old Kingdom, in which the first of the great pyramids—the tomb of the Third Dynasty king Djoser—was built at Saqqara (c. 2650 B.C.E.), followed soon after by the even more impressive ones at Giza, most notably that of King Khafre (2558–2532 B.C.E.). This was also the period of the Great Sphinx at Giza.

Sumerians versus Semites

Meanwhile, to the east, in Mesopotamia, as the nation-state of Egypt was emerging to the south, the Sumerians were creating a religious, legal, and architectural basis that would dominate the Fertile Crescent long after they faded into oblivion. The epic of Gilgamesh, the great ziggurats—stepped pyramidlike structures in honor of the gods—a complex legal system, and a complex mythological system were Sumerian inventions that would be adopted to some degree by the Semites who conquered them. Furthermore, for many centuries after the demise of the Sumerians their language would remain the vehicle of learning and culture in schools.

In the face of threats from the Semitic Akkadians in the north and the Elamites to the east, the various city-states of Sumer sometimes united as a federation during what is known as their Early Dynastic period. Frequent wars had led to a more centralized leadership of the various cities. The old positions of *en* or priest-king or -queen, spouse of the patron deity, and *lugal,* or military leader-protector, gradually merged into what was essentially a kingship by the end of the fourth millennium. And although there were general assemblies of all the states at Nippur and elsewhere, there was a strong tendency for these de facto kingdoms to fight among themselves. For a while the city of Kish under King Etana gained dominance over Sumer and over Semitic Akkad to the north. Then Uruk under such kings as Enmerkar, Lugalbanda, and Gilgamesh, all of whom became subjects of heroic legend, took its turn as the controlling power. Uruk's day was followed by that of Ur and later that of Lagash in about 2350 B.C.E. The brief Lagash dynasty is significant for the extensive archival material it collected. Whatever the Sumerian accomplishments, the battles between the city-states left the country open to attack and eventual conquest.

King Sargon I of Akkad conquered the region sometime between 2390 and 2330 B.C.E., establishing a capital, Agade (Akkad), near Kish. The Akkadians adapted their own Semitic language to cuneiform and it became the lingua franca of the region for centuries to come. The Akkadian dynasty controlled what was now, in effect, Sumer-Akkad, only until about 2254, when the old Sumerian area regained independence, beginning what is sometimes called the Neo-Sumerian period. King Naram-Sin of Akkad regained control of all of Mesopotamia soon after that, desecrating the holy city of Nippur, and he extended his territory to include the ancient Semitic kingdom of Ebla (perhaps the original Amorites) that had flourished in what is now northern Syria from c. 2700 B.C.E. Ebla is near Aleppo and not far from Harran, where Abraham (Abram) is said to have lived for a while on his way to Canaan. At Tell Mardikh, the site of Ebla's center, archeologists have found important materials, including what might be called the first bilingual dictionary, cuneiform tablets combining words in several languages.

Naram-Sin was deified by the Akkadians for his successes in Ebla and elsewhere, but eventually he lost power to invading Gutian tribes from the mountains of western Iran, who were in turn confronted by Utuhegal of Uruk and by Lagash, powerful again for a brief period under the *ensi* Gudea. Then, under Ur-Nammu of Ur, Sumer became independent once again, and the Third Dynasty of Ur, a renaissance period of education, literature, and elaborate law codes, dominated Sumer for about one hundred years beginning in about 2100 B.C.E. The Ur III dynasty ended when Ur was attacked by nomadic Semites, the Mardu, Amorites from the western desert. The Mardu settlements were looted and destroyed by Elamites from the east in about 2004 B.C.E. Ur III was followed by the Semitic dynasties of the cities Isin and Larsa (c. 2000–1763 B.C.E.), dynasties that considered themselves to be the preservers of the now ancient Sumerian culture.

Destabilization in Egypt

While the various entities of Mesopotamia were struggling with each other for hegemony, the Egyptian state was experiencing its own period of destabilization. The power of the god-king, indicated by the great pyramids at Dahshur and Giza, was being threatened by the middle of the millennium by an increase in the power of the priests and the noble class. With a partial decentralization of royal control came the rise of a kind of feudalism. This was also the period of the Pyramid Texts, elaborate recordings in royal tombs of hymns, prayers, and lists that reveal much of Egyptian culture at the time, especially of the dominant cult surrounding death and the afterlife, a cult centered on the god Osiris. By 2250 B.C.E. political anarchy threatened the state, and soon the Old Kingdom came to an end and the country broke into two kingdoms, with capitals at Memphis or Herakleopolis in the north (near modern Cairo) and Thebes (modern Luxor) in the south. At about the turn of the millennium, roughly coinciding with the fall of Ur in the north, Egypt was reunited by the Theban king Mentuhotep under the high god Amun, thus beginning the Middle Kingdom.

The Rise of Old Babylonia

The second millennium B.C.E. saw many changes in the Middle East. Early in the millennium Amorites (the name means "westerners"), Semites who had begun to migrate to the Fertile Crescent in the middle of the previous millennium, perhaps from the Arabian Peninsula, became powerful in Mesopotamia, Egypt, and the Levant (now Lebanon, Syria, Jordan, Israel, and Palestine). In Syria they established the city of Mari, and in Mesopotamia a capital, Babylon, in what had once been Akkad. Under Hammurabi (c. 1792–1750 B.C.E.), who ruled over a land populated by a variety of races, they developed a unifying code of laws and inscribed it on the famous column at Susa for all to see. Old Babylonia, as it is now called, was constantly threatened from within and by Elamites and others from outside its borders. Much of the area that had once been Sumer declared its independence during the rule of Hammurabi's son, and that area's kings stressed cultural descent from Sumer, even though the people who actually spoke Sumerian were now essentially extinct. But the decisive blow came when in 1600 B.C.E. Old Babylonia was invaded and defeated by the Hittites, Indo-Europeans from the northwest.

Hittites and Hurrians

Beginning early in the second millennium B.C.E. the Hittites had ruled over a large portion of Anatolia (Asian Turkey) that had previously been occupied by the non-Indo-European Hattians, a name used by the Hittites to identify themselves. In fact, the original Hattian culture is sometimes referred to as proto-Hattian to distinguish it from the later Hattian-Hittite culture. The Hittite arrival in Anatolia, perhaps as early as 2300 B.C.E., coincided with that of less powerful Indo-Europeans, including the Luwians and Palaians. The Hittites quickly adapted their language to the cuneiform script learned, presumably, from the Mesopotamians, and Hittite remained the dominant language of Anatolia during the second millennium.

The Hittites were progressive rulers in the sense that they accepted the languages, religions, and other cultural traditions that existed in the lands they conquered. From the Hattians and other neighbors, the Hurrians, they borrowed and assimilated so much of both languages and religions that it is difficult to speak of Hattian, Hurrian, and Hittite mythology and almost necessary to combine all three under the term *Anatolian*.

The so-called Hittite Old Kingdom was centered in Hattusa (near modern Boğazköy) and by the middle of the millennium had formed an empire of all of Anatolia and much of Mesopotamia. During the Middle Kingdom, between 1500 and 1380 B.C.E., however, Hattusa was ruled by kings with Hurrian names. That fact suggests possible conquest by the Hurrian kingdom of Mitanni, southwest of Lake Van in what is now the Kurdish area where Syria, Turkey, and Iraq meet. The Mitanni Hurrians (also known as Naharin), with their capital at Wassukkani, were themselves ruled by an Indo-Aryan aristocracy with some allegiance to Indian deities (Campbell, *Occidental*, 121).

The Hurrians, or Hurri, who were neither Indo-European nor Semitic, had moved into Mesopotamia and what is now Syria at about the time of the Hittite arrival in Anatolia. By the middle of the millennium they had established major centers at Nuzi in the eastern Tigris region and Alalakh in northern Syria, and by late in the millennium there was an important Hurrian presence and influence in Canaanite Ugarit.

In the mid-fourteenth century B.C.E. Hittite kings retook the throne in Hattusa, beginning the Early Empire period, and soon conquered the Mitanni Hurrians and established control over much of the Hurrian Empire in Mesopotamia and Syria. The Hittites had always been a warlike people who both traded and fought over the centuries with their neighbors the Hurrians and Assyrians, but also with the Babylonians and especially the Egyptians to the south. The

Egyptians considered them barbarians who, toward the end of the millennium, stood in the way of their imperial advance to the north and east. In 1300 the armies of the Hittites and the Egyptians fought to a draw near Kadesh, and eventually a treaty between Ramses II and Hattusili III was solidified by the marriage between the Egyptian pharaoh and Hattusili's daughter.

The Assyrians and Other Invaders

In about 1170 B.C.E. Hattusa fell to invaders, probably the so-called Sea People, an Indo-European group likely of Aegean or southern European origin from the west, and the Hittite time in history essentially came to an end. When the Hittites abandoned Babylonia, the Kassites, other Indo-Europeans from the eastern mountains, moved in and ruled for some time, but they were always challenged by the Assyrians, a Semitic people who had established trading colonies in the north of Mesopotamia late in the third millennium and who by 2300 B.C.E. had become a small kingdom of which the capital was Assur. Assur had been conquered by Sargon of Akkad in 2300 but had regained independence with the fall of the Ur III dynasty, only to be reconquered by Amorites and Hurrians. But when the Hurrian Empire collapsed in about 1360, the Assyrians once again became independent and maintained that independence in wars against not only the Hurrians but the Kassites. In 1225 B.C.E. the Assyrians, under King Tukulti-Ninurta (Nimrod), defeated the Kassites and briefly took over Babylon. A rebellion and a series of invasions by the Sea People led to the withdrawal of the Assyrians back to the north and the return of the Kassites to Babylon before they in turn were defeated by the Elamites, who took the much fought-over statue of the Babylonian city god Marduk as booty to Elam. At the end of the millennium King Nebuchadnezzar I of Isin liberated Babylonia from Elam and brought back the Marduk statue.

Egypt: The New Kingdom

The end of the reign of Hammurabi and the high point of Hittite imperialism had coincided with the invasion of Egypt by an Asiatic people referred to as Hyksos, who conquered much of the country, essentially putting an end to the Middle Kingdom and beginning an intermediate period in Egyptian history. But with their defeat at the hands of a Theban dynasty loyal to the god Amun-Re, the New Kingdom was born and a period of Egyptian expansion and artistic achievement followed under the leadership of Thothmose I and II, the latter's wife, Hatshepsut, Thothmose III, and especially Amenhotep III (1417–1366 B.C.E.), who extended the empire into parts of Mesopotamia and most of Canaan (modern Israel-Palestine and neighboring lands). The successor to Amenhotep II was his son Akhenaton (1366–1347 B.C.E.), known best for his attempt to introduce a monotheism based on the sun god (the Aton), with himself and his wife, Nefertiti, as the principal intermediaries between that divinity and mortals. He created a new capital city, Akhetaton (modern Tell el-'Amârna), north of Thebes. The next pharaoh was the boy Tutankhamen, under whose reign the old Amun religion was restored.

3

The Iron Age

The Hebrews

During the turmoil surrounding Akhenaton's religious revolution, Egypt gradually lost its hold on Canaan. Diplomatic letters of the period indicate a concern among Egyptians about the presence of Habiru or Apiru (essentially, "foreigners") under their jurisdiction who were irritants, and topographical lists of Amenhotep III and Ramses II refer to "the land of nomads [of] Yahweh" to the east of the delta in Sinai (Weinfeld, 483). The earliest reference to Israel itself comes in the reign of Merneptah, the son of Ramses II (Lesko, "Egyptian Religion," 45). It is possible that the term *Habiru*, which seems to have referred to several tribes, including the future Israelite Hebrews, became *Hebrew* and that in the situation surrounding these people we have the basis for the biblical story of the Exodus. In any case, it seems likely enough that nomadic herders of various tribes who were unified by varying degrees of kinship and by a religion, inspired perhaps by conflicts with Egyptian culture, wandered out of northern Egypt, where Semitic non-Egyptian tribes had lived for some time. These tribes would have moved into Canaan in about 1250 B.C.E. In support of this scenario are Egyptian documents suggesting that some of the Habiru were slaves who ran away and were pursued (Weinfeld, 484). When and how these tribes had first come to Egypt is unclear. It is possible that, as the biblical accounts suggest, they were the descendants of nomads who wandered from Mesopotamia early in the second millennium into Canaan and then to Egypt, perhaps fleeing drought and famine.

The Canaanites

The middle of the second millennium had seen the flourishing of major Canaanite centers along the Mediterranean coast, centers roughly contemporaneous with those of the Mycenaeans in Greece. Some of these centers grew out of ancient Stone Age settlements. Cities such as Byblos (in modern Lebanon) had by the beginning of the third millennium long been carrying on active trade with Egyptians and Mesopotamians. *Canaanite* is a somewhat vague term that has referred to the indigenous Semitic peoples of the "land of Canaan" into which Hebrews migrated late in the second millennium. In this sense Canaanites are simply pre-Hebrew Northwestern Semites and are related, for instance, to the Phoenicians (the term is used by some scholars simply to differentiate Iron Age from Bronze Age Canaanites). Certainly what we think of as Canaanite mythology is similar to that of the Phoenicians. The Phoenicians lived in the coastal area that is modern Lebanon. They invented the alphabet in about 1500 B.C.E., not long before the Mycenaeans in Greece overpowered the old Minoan civilization of Crete. The Phoenicians established colonies and trade connections throughout the Mediterranean world. Even the Mari-based Amorites are seen by some as Canaanites, but more often as proto-Arameans, the Arameans being the Semitic peoples who would settle around Aram (near present-day Damascus, in Syria) but who maintained a language and religion that were very different from those of other Semites in the area. More often—particularly in connection with religion and mythology—Canaanites are equated with the people of the city of Ugarit (Ras Shamra in modern Syria), where important texts dating from the fourteenth and thirteenth centuries B.C.E. have been found. Phoenicians have been more specifically associated with the Iron Age sea-trading culture that is centered in coastal cities such as Byblos, Tyre, and Sidon (all in modern Lebanon).

Wars in Canaan

The emergence of the Hebrew people in Canaan coincided roughly with invasions all over the Middle East of the Sea People mentioned above, who had much to do with the deterioration of both the Hittite and Egyptian empires and who in Canaan became known as the Philistines. It is of interest to note that the events of this period are roughly contemporaneous with those of the Trojan War on the western Anatolian coast, if such a war in fact took place. After destroying the city of Ugarit and other Canaanite centers and establishing their own state with cities such as Gaza and Ekron in what is now southern coastal Israel, the Philistines would gradually assimilate much of the indigenous Canaanite culture, including language and mythology. The name of their state, *Philistia*, would evolve still later into *Palestine*, the term eventually used for southern Canaan.

The late-second-millennium-B.C.E. Hebrew influx into Canaan is shrouded in mystery. This is because at first it was too insignificant in size to have much impact when compared to more unified and larger cultures such as the Assyrian, Egyptian, or Hittite. Furthermore, as in the case of earlier events — those surrounding the patriarch Abraham, for instance — what information we have about the Exodus from Egypt is deeply imbedded in biblical tradition containing many elements that are clearly mythical rather than historical. These stories can best be treated mythologically in a later chapter.

What can be said with some assurance is that the early Hebrews in Canaan, whether before or after the migration of the 1200s B.C.E., would have been a loosely related group of seminomadic tribes whose livelihood came from herding and occasional farming. Kinship groups would have been ruled by male heads of family and in some cases would have worshiped family or clan deities. According to Jewish tradition, the clans as a whole traced their ancestry from Abraham to the patriarch Jacob, whose name was changed to Israel, which made the Hebrews the children of Israel. The Hebrews who came to Canaan would have interacted with other Semitic groups — Edomites, Moabites, Midianites, and Ammonites, for example. The new migrants would have settled inland, as the coastal plains would have been populated by the various Canaanites, although some of the new-comers did apparently move into Canaanite cities, including the city that would become Jerusalem. It seems likely that the Hebrews both fought against and learned from the people around them. At first non-literate, they learned the language of the Canaanites and adopted their writing skills. Canaanite religion was attractive to some of the Hebrews, but so was the Yahweh religion, learned perhaps originally from the Midianites, who have sometimes been thought to be the remnants of the Hyksos people, who had once controlled and then been expelled from Egypt. Whatever the source, the Hebrews in all likelihood mixed with other tribes before and during the migration and adopted the Yahweh religion. That religion became the basis of what they saw as their God-given right as the nation of Israel to the land of Canaan.

The Rise of Israel

It was the struggle for settlement land against the indigenous Canaa-nites, the smaller immigrant tribes, and especially the Philistines that led to the cohesion of the Hebrews into a military power. At the end of the eleventh century B.C.E. the Hebrew clans united behind a monarchy. The first king of Israel was said to be Saul, who suffered several defeats at the hands of the Philistines. Saul was followed by David, of the clan of Judah, in about 1010 B.C.E. King David defeated the Moabites, the Edomites, the Ammonites, and the Arameans, as well as other Canaanite and Philistine rivals. He established his capi-tal at the Canaanite (specifically Jebusite) city of Jebus (Jerusalem) and during a forty-year reign was greatly responsible for what is known as the Golden Age of Israel.

Early in the first millennium, soon after the death of David, Solomon became the priest-king of Israel, and although tolerant of the religions of the indigenous people, he built a great temple for Yahweh in Jerusalem. In connection with Solomon we get a glimpse of the Arab culture in the south of the Arabian Peninsula in the visit by the queen of Saba (Sheba) to Jerusalem (2 Chronicles 9:1–12). Soon after Solomon's death in about 928 B.C.E. a civil war erupted and two states emerged—Israel in the north and Judah, with Jerusalem as its capital, in the south. Meanwhile, the greater empire established by David and Solomon was already in the process of disintegration. The Arameans and Edomites had rebelled in Solomon's time, and now both Israel and Judah were threatened by the rising Assyrian power from Mesopotamia. In the mid-ninth century B.C.E., under King Ahab, Israel, in alliance with the Arameans and the Phoenicians, first defeated and then, after infighting with the Arameans, was defeated by the Assyrians.

The Neo-Assyrians

For some time, beginning at the turn of the millennium, the Assyrians had been a potent force in the Middle East. In fact, the first half of the first millennium B.C.E. is usually referred to as the Neo-Assyrian period. Assyrian power became particularly formidable under a self-proclaimed king, Tiglath-Pileser III, who took power in Assur in 745 B.C.E. With an advanced Iron Age army, including huge battering devices and a cavalry of archers, the Assyrians defeated the Arameans of Syria and in 721 Israel. According to their custom, as a way of preventing future rebellions or the reestablishment of defeated nations, the Assyrians took away thousands of Israelites as slaves. Judah, too, was besieged, but Jerusalem was spared in return for a large ransom. Soon the Assyrians had conquered Egypt, which had weakened after internal struggles. In 671 they captured Memphis, and in 663 Assurbanipal conquered and sacked Thebes. By 640 B.C.E. the Assyrian Empire covered Mesopotamia, Egypt, Palestine, Syria, and much of Asia Minor. Judah survived as a puppet state under King Manasseh. During his reign the Yahweh religion shared space with that of the Assyrians and Canaanites.

The later years of the Assyrian Empire saw the building of roads, bridges, and complex water systems as well as the development of law courts and great cultural centers such as the library at Nineveh. The empire suffered at the end, however, from a civil war between the brothers Assurbanipal, whose base was Nineveh, and Shamash-shum-ukin, who ruled the area around Babylon.

The Neo-Babylonians and the Babylonian Exile

In 612 B.C.E. the Assyrians, in alliance with the Egyptians, were defeated by Medes from Persia, and Babylonians. Nineveh was destroyed, and under King Nebuchadnezzar II (605–562 B.C.E.) of the Chaldean dynasty, Babylon once again dominated the Middle East during an era known as the Neo-Babylonian. This was the period of the Hanging Gardens of Babylon and of great astronomical advancement as well as of a revival of Babylonian religion and mythology that reached back to the ancient Sumerians. It was also the period of the Babylonian captivity, or exile.

King Nebuchadnezzar II made several forays into Judah, each time setting up puppet regimes and taking away prominent Judeans into captivity in Babylon. In this way, like the Assyrians before him, he hoped to prevent future rebellions and the reestablishment of hostile regimes within his empire. During the last attack on Jerusalem in 586 B.C.E. he sacked the city, destroyed the temple, and took away the rebellious puppet king and still more Judeans.

It was during the Babylonian exile that the captives from Judah emerged fully as Jews in the religious sense. Unlike earlier Israelite captives of the Assyrians, the Babylon Hebrews were not forced to become assimilated into the dominant culture. The first books of what in a fifth-century-B.C.E. collation would become the Hebrew Bible, the Torah, had been written down from earlier oral sources in Israel and Judah possibly as early as the tenth century but probably not until the ninth or even eighth centuries B.C.E. With these stories as a foundation, many of the Hebrews in exile developed rules of conduct and prayers to support the exclusive Yahweh religion, which gave them identity. The way was clearly paved for the development of synagogue worship and the emergence of rabbinical interpretation and authority.

4

◈

Jews, Christians, and Muslims

Indo-European Rulers and the Jews

When the Persians under Cyrus conquered Babylon in 539 B.C.E. many of the Babylonian Israelites migrated "home" to Jerusalem and eventually rebuilt the city walls and the Temple. Others remained in Babylon, where a Jewish community flourished for several centuries. Those who came to Jerusalem did so with Persian approval; in Cyrus's Zoroastrian view Yahweh was among the deities on the side of good in the struggle between good and evil in the universe. Most important, the new arrivals in Jerusalem came as committed Jews rather than as Judeans or as Hebrews influenced, as they had been earlier, by the myths and religious ways of the indigenous Canaanites. Judah became an exclusively Jewish theocratic state.

The Persian Empire under the Achaemenid dynasty in the Middle East included not only Babylonia and Palestine but also Egypt and much of Anatolia. The empire lasted until 333–331 B.C.E., when Persia was conquered by Alexander the Great of Macedonia. With Alexander's death at an early age in 323 the empire was divided up by his generals. The Ptolemies gained control in Egypt, the Seleucids and Parthians in Mesopotamia, Palestine, and Persia. Once again Palestine became a battlefield for rival factions from other lands. The Seleucids of Syria and the Ptolemies of Egypt took turns capturing Jerusalem seven times during the late fourth century B.C.E. When the

Seleucids desecrated the Temple in 168, a revolt led by the Maccabees, a dynasty of priests and kings, led to a brief period of independence for Judah.

Romans, Jews, and Christians

In 63 B.C.E. the Romans annexed Palestine and ruled the land both directly, through a Roman governor, and indirectly, through procurators such as Pontius Pilate in Judea (26–37 C.E.) and pro-Roman Jewish kings such as Herod the Great (37–4 B.C.E.). It was during Herod's reign, tradition tells us, that Jesus of Nazareth was born and during Pilate's reign that he died. The mythologizing of aspects of this Jewish reformer's life would be essential to what would become Christianity, the second of the monotheistic faiths to trace its origins to Abraham.

In 66 C.E. the Jews rebelled against Roman rule, as they would later in Cyprus and Egypt. In 70 C.E. the Temple was destroyed, and soon after that large numbers of Jews were forced out of Palestine.

The next years and centuries saw the development of various forms of religion springing directly or indirectly from the Jewish source. The rapid development of rabbinical Judaism, marked by the compilation of the Mishnah (interpretations of the Torah) and later by sections of the Talmud (a collection consisting of the Mishnah and the Gemara, commentary on the Mishnah), took place in Palestine and Babylonia. Gnosticism and Christian monasticism (the "Desert Fathers") emerged in Egypt, and Manichaeism, which was a blend of Christianity, Gnosticism, and Zoroastrianism, blossomed in Mesopotamia. Christianity in general was gaining a foothold throughout the Middle East. But the period was also one of Roman persecution of Christians and Jews throughout the empire. Christian persecutions came to an end when the emperor Constantine announced his Edict of Toleration in 312 C.E. The persecution of Jews, however, continued, and early in the fourth century C.E. the Christian presence in Jerusalem was dominant. In 330 a new eastern capital of the empire, Constantinople (old Byzantium, modern Istanbul), was dedicated, and in 337 Constantine was baptized. By late in the century Christianity was the official religion of the Roman Empire, and the Middle East was dominated by Christian-Byzantine power.

In the fifth century C.E. both Judaism, through the continuing process of Talmudic editing and rabbinical teaching, and Christianity, through a series of Church councils held mostly in the Middle East, were engaged in a process of doctrinal, scriptural, and liturgical foundation building. In the sixth century Christian dominance and Christian persecution of Jews both in the Middle East and in Europe continued. The seventh century, however, gave birth to a religious movement that would also claim origins in the Semitic patriarch Abraham and that would challenge both of its Abrahamic predecessors for centuries to come. This was the religion of Islam, which accompanied the influx of Arabs and Arab culture in the Middle East.

The Arabs

Muslims consider the pre-Islamic age as the *jahiliyah,* or "age of ignorance"—that is, time before the revelations of Allah (*al-ilah,* "the god") to his prophet Muhammad. The Arabs were Semitic peoples of the Arabian Peninsula, who spoke a language closely related to the languages of the Palestinian and Mesopotamian Semites, including, of course, the Hebrews. Arab culture, like that of the early Hebrews, would have been centered in kinship, clans, and tribes. Their presence as organized groups in the peninsula has been dated as early as 1200 B.C.E. The queen of Saba's visit to King Solomon in Jerusalem would have been early in the first millennium B.C.E. Sabaeans are listed in Assyrian documents by the eighth century B.C.E. Inscriptions describe an outpost in Ethiopia in the fifth century B.C.E., and Sabaeans are mentioned by classical writers beginning in the fourth century B.C.E. The fertile land of the southern peninsula, known in ancient times as Arabia Felix, in what is now Yemen, gave rise to several centers of commerce, trade, and culture in addition to Saba, which gradually gained ascendancy over the others. These were city-states ruled by priest-kings (*mukarribs*) or kings (*maliks*). Among the more important states were Ma'in, Qataban, and Hadhramaut.

Intertribal warfare and religions of many idols would have been characteristic of the earliest history of the Arabs. The Bedouin tribes of the midpeninsula—around the regions of Hijaz (containing Mecca and Medina) and Najd (containing Riyadh)—were constantly at war. But even early on there appears to have been a sense of pan-Arabism, as indicated by a tradition of annual gatherings of tribes for poetry competitions—a kind of poetic Olympic Games—and the development of a common way of life based on the concept of *muruwah*. *Muruwah* obligated a man to obey his overlord, or *sayyid*, and to accept the communal ideal of the blood feud, in which revenge for murder could be taken on any member of the murderer's tribe as a substitute for the murderer himself. In general, *muruwah* also provided a sense of the importance of community as opposed to the individual, of generosity as opposed to material need. All of these concepts would be important for the later emergence of Islam.

By the time of Muhammad Arabia had long been taken advantage of by various powers. Persians from an early date had controlled the area around Saba. Although there had been Arab kingdoms as far north as Syria and Iraq—one was led by Queen Zenobia—they were annexed by the Romans in the second and third centuries C.E. Later, Byzantine Christians would establish Christian-Arab kingdoms in Syria and Iraq and elsewhere in the Middle East. Not long before Muhammad's birth, Christian Abyssinians had come up from Yemen and invaded Mecca.

The Muslims

Muhammad ibn Abdallah was born about 570 C.E. into the Quraysh tribe of the Hijaz region of Arabia. He was a merchant in the city of Mecca and was obsessed by the idea that his tribe had sacrificed old values for new materialistic ones. Gradually Muhammad came to believe that the old Arabic concept of divinity, *al-ilah*—associated with the strange cube-shaped structure in the center of Mecca, the Kabah—was the one true god, the same god as that of the Jews and Christians. Muhammad believed that Allah conveyed to him the possibility of tribal redemption in words that became, through him, in Arabic, the Muslim holy book, the Qur'an (Koran).

Like Jesus, Muhammad began to preach the Word, and like Jesus, he thought of himself as a reformer for his own people, one who would revitalize and give new life to the old religion. Like most prophets, he was rejected by his own people, and so began a struggle with the pagan population of Mecca and an alliance with the more sympathetic people of Medina, a city some 250 miles away. By the time of his death in 632, Muhammad had achieved a remarkable unity—an *ummah*, or community, that essentially united all of the previously warring Arab tribes. Recognized as the true messenger or final prophet of God, Muhammad had become the de facto founder of a new religion, Islam, as Jesus had several centuries earlier become the de facto founder of Christianity.

At first Muslims maintained good relations with the older Abrahamic monotheists, fellow "peoples of the Book," but struggles with Christians and Jews, who shared the Islamic sense of exclusivity, were inevitable. Like that of the Jews especially, the nationalism of the Arabs was a tribal and religious nationalism for which certain compromises were impossible. Before long, in spite of internal struggles between factions such as the Umayyads and the Abbasids, led by different caliphs (secular and religious heads of state), Muslim armies, now no longer exclusively Arab, advanced in all directions, forming a great empire that would take in all of the Middle East, including Egypt and Persia. Muslim armies would later move east and west, conquering much of the world, including parts of Christian Europe, where the Ottoman army was finally stopped at the gates of Vienna in 1683. Muslims controlled the Iberian peninsula from the eighth to the fifteenth centuries.

The Crusaders

European Christians had long seen the march of Islam as both a territorial and religious threat. Holy wars against Muslims took place almost from the earliest period of Muslim expansion—in Spain, in Sicily, and in the Byzantine struggle for survival against the Turks. The fall of Jerusalem to the Selkuk Turks in 1077 set off waves of horror among Christians. Armed crusaders set out in waves to liberate Jerusalem and the "Holy Land" as a whole from the infidel during the twelfth and thirteenth centuries. Several crusades led to varying degrees of success, but failure usually followed. In 1229, for instance, Frederick II of Hohenstaufen won a victory and had himself crowned king of Jerusalem, but the city was retaken in 1244. Muslims ruled essentially all of the Middle East for several centuries after that.

The Modern Period

After the defeat of the Ottomans at Vienna in the seventeenth century, Muslim power was diminished. The advent of European colonialism occurred in the eighteenth century and continued on in various degrees until the years following World War II, when a still deeper rift developed between the Muslim Middle East and the West. With the formation of the state of Israel in what Arabs saw as their land, the rift became more profound and more specifically oriented. In 1967 Jews once again took power in the West Bank, which includes eastern Jerusalem, the "Old City," containing most of the Jewish, Christian, and Muslim holy sites. Today the struggle between Semitic peoples for the city that is holy to the three Abrahamic religions and for the land that was once Canaan is still running its course.

Another example of modern struggles reflecting ancient ones exists in Iraq. Saddam Hussein's political use of ancient Mesopotamian mythology and history, suggesting himself as a natural successor to the likes of Sargon of Akkad and Hammurabi of Babylonia, is common knowledge. It is impossible to avoid the seemingly inherent divisions that continue to plague the area, even within the context of a single religion, Islam. Where there was a north-south conflict between Assyrians and Babylonians and Akkadians and Sumerians, we now have Kurds opposed to Arab Iraqis and Sunni Muslims against Shiite Muslims with divisions enforced by outside powers. Furthermore, the war between Iraq and Iran in the 1980s points back to ancient wars between Mesopotamians and Elamites and other Persians from the east (Iran).

Part Two

THE MYTHOLOGIES

5

The Mythology of Prehistory

Until the advent of writing, Middle Eastern religions and myths, like those of other parts of the world, can only be surmised by way of archeological remains such as shrines, paintings, figurines, and burial sites. From excavations of the earliest human sites, those of the Paleolithic period, little or nothing mythological or religious can be determined with any certainty. Neanderthal sites such as those at Shanidar in Mesopotamia, Mount Carmel in Palestine, and various places in Egypt reveal some care in burial practices—seemingly symbolic, even ritualistic arrangements of bodies and the placing of animals in graves with human corpses, perhaps suggesting either a sacrificial cult and/or a belief in an afterlife. It is possible that stories of the afterlife or sacrifice might have developed along with such cults and beliefs. The Natufian sites of Palestine and Syria dating from the Mesolithic period (c. 10,000–8,000 B.C.E.) provide slightly stronger evidence of religious storytelling. Among objects found in the Natufian excavations are figurines of embracing couples, suggesting the concept of the sacred marriage, a concept that would be important in the Neolithic period (see Srejovich, 354). Grave pits in association with grain storage pits indicate the possibility of a fertility cult associated with the early development of agriculture. Furthermore, animals buried with the dead and decorations applied

to corpses point to a belief in an afterlife, presumably with rele-
vant myths.

Things become clearer in the Neolithic period. An unusually
shaped room with a kind of altar niche in Jericho suggests a cult center or shrine, a precursor to the much larger fifth-millennium temple-
like structures at Ubaid sites in Mesopotamia. In the Euphrates
valley, early-eighth-century female figurines found at Mureybet and
Çayonu have led archeologists to hypothesize a specific goddess cult
associated with fertility and the earth itself. Somewhat later figurines
of a similar type have been found at Hacilar in Anatolia, also suggesting a fertility goddess mythology.

It is generally accepted that the source of the Neolithic fertility religion is the rapid development of agriculture and animal husbandry
during the period. Both required increasingly specialized community
activity that included ritual and myth to ensure productivity. A
priestly caste would have developed to watch over and lead religious
practices. It is reasonable to assume that planting and plant growth
gave rise to myths of death and regeneration. Metaphors are essential
to myth. Humans have always expressed the miracles of nature and
the universe in terms of what we know—human life. The agricultural
process was obviously analogous to human and animal fertilization,
gestation, and birth. A logical ancillary concept was that of sacrifice,
both in the sense of a gift to the mysterious source of life and in the
sense of a seed planted in the earth. It was clear that what dies and is
planted can come back in a new form, and from an early time death
turning to new life seems, from burial sites, to have applied to humans "planted" in graves.

Clearly the most important metaphor for fertility itself was sexuality in connection with the birth-giving female, and as agriculture partially displaced hunting as a primary food source, the woman would
have gained in stature. The emergence of polytheism, including sexually active gods—sometimes in the form of animals such as the bull
or the goat—presided over by a great goddess was inevitable. The
fertility of the woman was associated with the fertility of nature, and
nature itself—the earth—came to life in the metaphor of the earth
mother or earth goddess.

Çatal Hüyük

The most tantalizing evidence of a developed Neolithic mythology of this sort is at a site known as Çatal Hüyük, discovered in 1957 by archeologist James Mellaart on the Konya plateau in Anatolia. Çatal Hüyük is arguably the most revealing of prehistoric sites anywhere. A now familiar image from that site is the tiny terra-cotta figurine of a large woman seated between feline animals and apparently giving birth.

She is generally referred to as the "mother goddess," and while it is convenient and probably even correct to assume that identity for her, it is important to remember that without written documents we can know little of the specifics of her story; her genealogy and her name, if she was more than a generic entity, are a mystery. We can, of course, hypothesize about her comparatively by looking ahead to her descendants among literate cultures, recognized as such by their association with animals and with fertility. These would include, for example, Inanna in Mesopotamia and Isis in Egypt, both of whom will be discussed later. We can glean at least some direct knowledge of the Çatal

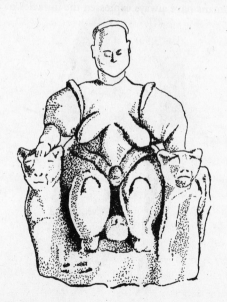

The Çatal Hüyük "mother goddess," c. 6000 B.C.E.

Hüyük goddess's deeds by way of the many wall paintings in buildings obviously intended as shrines and sanctuaries at the site.

The goddess is depicted not only as a mother but as a young girl and as an old woman, indicating her association with the year and with other cycles of nature. Sometimes she is associated with a bull, clearly a representation of the male principle. The bull, like the goddess, is depicted at various stages of life, in all likelihood representing seasonal and life-cycle changes in plants and humans. He is a tiny horned animal emerging at birth, and he is a mature and vibrant figure facing the goddess on a Çatal Hüyük sanctuary wall. In these roles he foreshadows later themes of the mother goddess and her son-lover.

Those who doubt a Neolithic understanding of the connection between sexual intercourse and birth would do well to consider one relief in a Çatal Hüyük shrine that depicts two figures—a male and a female—intimately embracing and immediately next to it a female figure holding an infant.

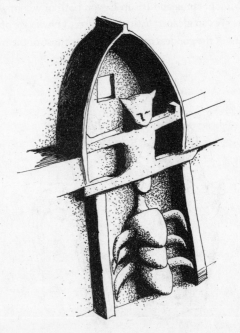

The birth of the bull god at Çatal Hüyük, c. 6000 B.C.E.

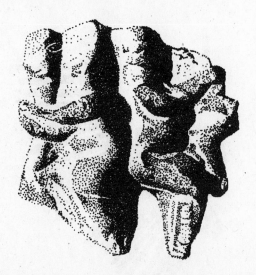

The Çatal Hüyük goddess with consort and with child, c. 6000 B.C.E.

Depictions of the goddess easily outnumber those of the male entity at Çatal Hüyük. One of the most startling representations looks forward to the later expressions of the necessary role of death in the fertility/regeneration process. Like the Indian goddess Devi in her form as the devouring Kali, the Çatal Hüyük mother goddess takes life back into her being in death even as she delivers it to the world in birth. In many Çatal Hüyük paintings the goddess is surrounded by plants, but in one early shrine she becomes many overpowering flying vultures who seem to have decapitated tiny humans (see figure on page 36).

In the Middle Neolithic (c. 5500–4500 B.C.E.) and the High Neolithic (c. 4500–3500 B.C.E.) agriculture and animal husbandry in the context of established settlements developed still further. Pottery and weaving became important. In the Samarra and Halaf pottery of Mesopotamia, female and bull figures mingle with abstract symbols. The cult of a sacrificed and resurrected bull god related to a dominant great goddess—sometimes with a cow's head—found its way to the Egyptian delta as well. In the Ubaid culture of southern Mesopotamia the ziggurat temples were first built at the site that would become Sumerian Ur.

The Çatal Hüyük goddess as vulture, c. 6000 B.C.E.

The ziggurats were capped by apparent sanctuaries that Joseph Campbell suggests were "for the ritual of the world-generating union of the earth goddess" and the descendant of the old bull god, "the lord of the sky." The earthly representatives of this couple would have been a queen and a king of a hieratic city or city-state (Campbell, *Primitive*, 144). This tradition of the sacred marriage is a central element in the religion and mythology of the first great civilization of written history, that of the Sumerians of Mesopotamia, whose culture emerged from or replaced that of the Ubaids.

6

The Mythology of
Mesopotamia

Just as Minoan, Mycenaean, Dorian, and Ionian myths are all part of what we think of as Greek mythology, with its diversity, its conflicting versions of particular events, and its literary as opposed to purely religious and folkloric content, Mesopotamian mythology is made up of the myths and religions of several cultures that over many centuries inhabited the same geographic area—essentially modern Iraq—and assimilated each other's religious understandings and stories. Mesopotamian mythology refers here to the period between the advent of writing in Sumer late in the fourth millennium B.C.E. and the emergence of Christianity in the first century C.E. The mythology in question in all likelihood reaches back in the oral tradition of the preliterate cultures of the area, but in terms of written records, it begins in Sumer and is absorbed and added to by Sumer's Semitic conquerors and successors, including the various Akkadian, Babylonian, and Assyrian dynasties. The mythology of the Hurrians and Hittites, whose presence in northern Mesopotamia was significant, will be treated in connection with Anatolian traditions.

Much of what we know of Mesopotamian mythology comes from mid- to late-third-millennium Sumerian and Akkadian tablet fragments, including a list of Old Sumerian gods from Fara (ancient Shuruppak, near Nippur) and Lagash dating from c. 2500–2300 B.C.E., as well as from scripts in Sumerian and Akkadian of Hammurabi's period and from the ruins of the seventh-century-B.C.E. Assurbanipal Library in Nineveh. The preservation of Sumerian language and mythology for some two thousand years after the essential demise of the Sumerians as a viable entity themselves is an indication of the importance of Sumer to Mesopotamian culture as a whole.

The Pantheons

The Mesopotamian pantheon that can be derived from the various sources is clearly based on the Sumerian model contained in the Old Sumerian or pre-Sargonic Fara god list, but aspects and identities of deities change from place to place and from era to era. Sometimes several gods become one or one divides into several. Collectively the deities are the Anuna (Anunnaki), the "royal ones." The names in parentheses below are Semitic (Akkadian) equivalents to the Sumerian originals unless otherwise indicated. The gods and goddesses of the pantheon as originally conceived were often personifications of natural phenomena or aspects of the cosmos, concepts rather than anthropomorphic beings. Often they were paired as male and female aspects of the same phenomenon. They tended to be associated with particular cities or areas and to reflect the characteristics of those areas. These were some of the most important gods and goddesses in the myths of the region.

Sumerian/Babylonian Deities

An (Anu or Anum) was the somewhat distant father god, an embodiment of the sky or heaven. He separated early on from his mate, Uras, later Ki, both personifications of earth, and in so doing made room for the universe. As the great bull, with his roar of thunder and especially his semen-rain, with which he fertilizes Ki, An seems to have been a mythological descendant of the Neolithic bull gods such as the one at Çatal Hüyük. In some cities he was seen as the sky husband of Antu (or Antum), the female version of the sky, who was, like so many ancient mother goddesses, bovine. Her milk flowed from cloud-udders and, like her husband's semen, fertilized the earth. The male An and the female Ki—heaven and earth—were thought in certain areas to be the offspring of the mother goddess Nammu, believed by some to have been the creatrix of humans. In a Babylonian version, An was born of the primordial couple Anshar and Kishar. An's Sumerian cult center was in Uruk. If at first he was the most powerful of the gods, he lost some of his importance over the centuries, giving way to the gods Enlil and Marduk and the goddess Inanna.

Enlil

Enlil (Ellil) was the storm, air, and wind (*lil*) lord (*en*) and the son of An. He was the only god other than An who could bestow the *me* (*parsu*)—the important elements of the Sumerian concept of divine civilized order—on other deities or on kings, temples, or cities. Like storm gods in other regions of the world—the Norse Thor, for example—Enlil was in some ways more important than the father god. His base was the holy city of Nippur—the Vatican of ancient Sumer—and from there during the Early Dynastic period he gave authority to Sumerian kings in the name of his father from his great protoziggurat temple E-kur (the name means "mountain house"). Enlil was linked in Babylon to his female equivalent, the wind or air-wind (*lil*) goddess or lady (*nin*), Ninlil (Mullissu), who before her marriage had been called Sud and occasionally was identified with the mother goddess Ninhursaga (Belitili), who, with An, Enlil, and Enki, was one of the four principal deities of Sumer. Ninhursaga, "mistress of the foothills" and later "mistress of the gods," represented fertility and birth; her sign included the uterus of a cow, associating her with Neolithic cow goddesses important to agriculture and animal husbandry. As the wife of Enlil, she was the mother of the seasons. Ninhursaga, as indicated above, was assimilated with various other goddesses, depending on the particular locale and era. Her sometime husband Enlil was the source of fertility and abundance as well as of storms, floods, and destruction. Some cities believed him to be the father of the goddess Inanna, who eventually made her way into what became the top five of Sumerian deities. One of Enlil's sons was Ninurta, the city god of Nippur, an agricultural rain god sometimes identified with the god Ningirsu. His sign was the plow, as that of his father, Enlil, was the hoe. At the yearly fertility festival the king of

Nippur opened the ceremonies behind a plow, in celebration of Nin-urta. Other sons of Enlil were the moon god Nanna (Suen, Sin), who with his wife, Ningal, was particularly worshiped at Ur. Nanna and Ningal were the parents of the sun god Utu (Shamash), the lord of judgment, and of the goddess Inanna. Still another son of Enlil (or of An) was the weather god Ishkur (Adad), sometimes the twin brother of the god Enki.

Enki

Enki (Ea) was one of the most important Mesopotamian gods. Lord (*en*) of the soil or earth (*ki*), whose home was the underground sweet waters (*abzu, apsu*), he was a god necessary to irrigation, a practice important in his home, the city of Eridu in the southern marshlands of what is present-day Iraq. Enki was a trickster of sorts, known for his magical powers and incantations. Wise and skillful at all crafts, he was usually said to be a son of An and the mother-riverbed goddess Nammu (the name means "lady vulva") and was considered third in rank among the deities after An and Enlil. Damgalnuna (Damkina), still another version of the mother goddess, was his wife. Their son Asarluhi was later assimilated in Babylon into the god Marduk. Like most trickster gods, Enki possessed an insatiable sexual appetite, a fact that probably was a metaphorical expression of his role as a god of fertility and irrigation.

Inanna

Eventually the most important of the Mesopotamian goddesses was Inanna (Ishtar), also known as Innin or Ninnin. In her primary center at Uruk, where dates were a staple crop, she was Ninana, "mistress of heaven" and "lady of the date clusters." Like many fertility goddesses, she was sometimes the "cow of heaven." In her assimilation with the Akkadian Semitic astral goddess Ishtar, she was called "mistress of the *me*," making her (with An and Enlil) one of the most powerful of deities. Depending on the tradition, Inanna was the daughter of Enlil, Nanna, or Enki. Above all, she was a goddess of sexuality and reproduction and was central to the ubiquitous Mesopotamian ritual of the sacred marriage. In hymns for these occasions she longs for and achieves intercourse with a king in order to bring fertility to the land. In Babylon Inanna could also play the role of a possibly dangerous femme fatale, as in the case of her attempt to seduce the hero Gilgamesh. Central to the most famous stories about her are her associations with a sister, Ereshkigal (Allatu), goddess of the underworld, and her relationship with the shepherd—sometimes fisherman—god Dumuzi (Tammuz in Hebrew and Aramaic). Dumuzi was represented by kings in the sacred marriage rites, especially at Uruk. As the husband of the "mistress of the date clusters," he was identified with a local god, Amaushumgalanna, the fertile power behind the date harvest. Later Dumuzi-Tammuz, whose myth involved his death, would merge with other dying gods of the Middle East.

What stands out about all of the gods whose origins are in Sumer is their association with agriculture and fertility. Although colorful myths about them developed, it seems clear that such myths were, like the principal characters in them, seen not so much as literal histories but as metaphors for natural phenomena and the practices of agriculture and animal husbandry.

Marduk

Other sorts of deities existed in Mesopotamia, especially city gods. Good examples are the eponymous Assyrian Assur and the god Marduk. Assur at various periods was assimilated with earlier gods. He was Enlil, Anshar—the sometime father of An—and eventually Marduk. Marduk is the central figure in the Babylonian creation epic, the *Enuma Elish*. As in the case of Assur, his nature was associated not with fertility in particular but with the rise of the city-state of which he was the patron. He came into his own with the rise to power of Hammurabi early in the second millennium B.C.E. Although he existed in earlier texts and was even said to be the son of Ea (Enki), Marduk was essentially created as a "new" god in Babylon. According to the priests of that city, Anu (An) and Ellil (Enlil) gave him suzerainty over human society, and in popular tradition he, along with his father, Ea, and the sun god Shamash (Utu), was considered to be a deity accessible in prayer, one who cared about human beings and their problems. Marduk's popularity grew during the various political developments in Babylonia, and over the centuries his cult spread in Mesopotamia, until by the twelfth century B.C.E., as indicated in the *Enuma Elish*, he was considered to be king not only of humans but of the gods themselves. His power was indicated by his depiction as a young bull.

Kassite Deities

As conquerors of parts of Mesopotamia, the Kassites brought local gods with them, but these deities either did not survive for long or were assimilated into the gods of the area. Thus a Kassite form of Enlil or An was Harbe. The Kassite Burias was equated with the Sumerian weather god Ishkur (Adad). Surias or Sah was Utu (Shamash), and Maruttas was Ninurta (Black and Green, 112).

Elamite Deities

The Elamites of Persia honored the Mesopotamian deities but also introduced their own into that pantheon. These included (among many others about whom little is known) the mother goddess Pienenkir, Nahhunte the sun god, Napir the moon god, and the sky god Humban, perhaps a form of the Mesopotamian Huwawa (Humbaba), Enlil's monstrous guardian of the Cedar Forest who plays an important role in the story of Gilgamesh (Black and Green, 74–75, 106).

Mesopotamian Cosmic Myths

The Sumerian Creation

In *Sumerian Mythology*, Samuel Noah Kramer outlines the Sumerian creation as found in a series of fragments, some of which he calls "Gilgamesh, Enkidu, and the Netherworld" (30). He points out that the Sumerian term for the universe was *an-ki* (41), literally the combination of An (heaven) and Ki (earth), which emerged as a primordial mountain from the maternal subterranean waters of the goddess Nammu. An and Ki, as male and female, conceived Enlil and, presumably, the other Anunnaki. As in many creation myths, heaven and earth had to be separated from each other in order that further creation could take place between them. So it was that the sky god, An, raised the sky and the area of heaven above it, and the air god, Enlil, took his mother, the earth, down, leaving the appropriate space. The goddess Ereshkigal was sent to be queen of the underworld. The gods and goddesses married, were fruitful, and took responsibility for the various aspects of agriculture. The work of farming was difficult, however, and the gods began grumbling, especially as the crafty god Enki, son of Nammu herself, lay sleeping while they worked.

Nammu had the idea of waking up her son and suggesting that he create humans (to work in the fields). Enki delegated the job to Nammu, instructing her to take some clay from the marshes (*abzu*, later *apsu*) in which he lay and to shape the clay into figures. The created humans were put to work under the watchful eyes of the goddess Ninmah-Ninhursaga.

Enki and Ninmah

To celebrate their newfound freedom and the creation of humans, the Anunnaki had a banquet at which Enki and Ninmah drank too much. Ninmah challenged Enki to a creative contest. She would make new humans with any defects she saw fit. Enki agreed but with the idea that he would attempt to choose roles for the misfits that would negate their defects. A man with an eye problem he made a singer. A man who constantly leaked semen he cured with a magic water incantation. There were six such creations and "cures." Then the combatants changed positions. Enki would create humans with defects for Ninmah to counteract. One of these was a being called an *umul* who was so helpless that it could neither talk, walk, nor feed himself. Taunted by Enki to solve the being's problems, Ninmah asked it questions that it could not answer and offered it food that it could not use its hands to hold. Finally she gave up in disgust. Enki had won the contest. At least one scholar has suggested reasonably that the *umul* was probably the first infant (see Leick, 43).

Enki and Ninhursaga

This is a myth that gives expression to Enki's ancient metaphorical aspect as the power behind the irrigation complexities of the southern marshlands. Enki lived in and was clearly associated with the sweet underground waters (*abzu, apsu*), which later would themselves be personified in Babylon as the god Apsu.

Enki's phallus, we are told, filled the ditches "with semen," that is, water—the words are the same in Sumerian—in the tradition of the father god, An, whose semen was life-giving rain (Wolkstein and Kramer, 139). Married to Damgalnuna (the name means "true wife"), one of several mother goddesses, Enki nevertheless "directed his semen owed to Damgalnuna . . . into the womb of Ninhursag[a]." When that goddess gave birth to the beautiful Ninmu, also a form of the mother goddess, Enki "poured semen into [her] womb." Ninmu gave birth to the goddess Ninkurra (meaning "mistress of the land"), and Enki fertilized her womb, causing the birth of Uttu (meaning "vegetation"). When Enki wished to pour his semen into Uttu, Ninhursaga advised the girl to resist unless Enki could bring her cucumbers, apples, and grapes. Enki obliged by reaching out and fertilizing more dry zones, which then produced these new products. Delighted, Uttu took Enki to "her lap," and he "poured the semen into the womb." But Ninhursaga wiped excess semen from the young goddess's body—the body of "vegetation"—and created eight new plants. In order to name these plants—that is, to declare their fates—Enki had first to eat them. This act so angered Ninhursaga that she cursed Enki, saying he would die, and then she disappeared, leaving the gods—the Anunnaki—sitting in despair "in the dust." Presumably the dust signifies that the land had dried up, deprived of Ninhursaga's fertile presence and of Enki's vital fluids, eight parts of his body now in a sense being clogged by the eight plants he had eaten. It was a little fox who determined a way of bringing the great goddess back. She returned and cured Enki by "fix[ing]" him "in her vulva" and naming eight new deities to counteract the poisoning by the plants.

Enlil and Ninlil

In a Sumerian myth from Nippur discovered in Old and Middle Babylonian and Neo-Assyrian tablets, a myth that bears similarities to the Enki stories of seduction, the god Enlil is attracted to his natural counterpart, the young and beautiful Ninlil. Her mother, realizing that

Ninlil is pubescent, advises her to purify herself in the river but to avoid the canal (irrigation ditch) called Inunbirdu, where Enlil will be lurking, ready to seduce and impregnate her. Naturally, Ninlil goes directly to the canal. Enlil is, in fact, waiting there, and he begins to attempt the seduction. Ninlil at first resists, but later Enlil finds her at a more hidden place and rapes her, engendering the moon god Nanna (Suen or Sin). For this act, or perhaps because Ninlil had not had time for the ritual of purification, he (or his son Nanna) seems to have been expelled by the "fifty great gods," perhaps to the underworld. Enlil leaves but is followed by Ninlil, and in various disguises he impregnates her with gods who may possibly take his or Nanna's place in the underworld. In any case, the myth ends with a hymn to Enlil as the source of abundance and fertility.

Enlil and Sud

In another version of the Enlil-Ninlil myth, also discovered in Babylonian and Neo-Assyrian fragments, Enlil, who is looking for a wife, meets the beautiful Sud. Enlil's advances are not accepted, but later he sends an envoy from Nippur to ask Sud's mother for the girl's hand. Through his agent, he gives Sud a secret love gift and promises her mother that her daughter will rule with him. At the suggestion of the mother, he sends his sister Aruru-Ninmah with a huge assortment of gifts—jewels, of course, but especially fruits of the earth. In a ritual in Enlil's temple Sud's face is anointed with holy oil, and the couple consummates the sacred marriage on the "shining bed." Finally, Enlil renames Sud—that is, he pronounces her fates or her essences—as Nintu (the "lady of birth"), Asnan (meaning "grain"), and Ninlil, his natural complement or queen.

Ninurta and Ninhursaga

In this myth, also called Lugale, Ninurta (also Ningirsu), who in some places was the "firstborn of Enlil" and son of Ninhursaga (of whom Ninlil, as a grain and birth goddess, could be a version), wages a preemptive war against his enemy Azag. Enlil sends a torrential downpour to defeat Azag, leaving Ninurta free to build a *hursag*, a natural dam (the foothills), and so direct irrigation waters into the Tigris valley. Ninurta-Ningirsu then honors his mother by renaming her Ninhursaga (the "lady of the foothills").

Inanna and Enki

In a myth dating probably from the end of the third millennium B.C.E., the goddess Inanna, lacking any particular office or function among the gods, decides to visit the crafty Enki in the *abzu* at his home in Eridu with the intention of stealing the powerful elements of the *me*. The *me* are the sources of Sumerian civilized order inherent originally in the primal waters, the great goddess Nammu. They include, for example, ritual, priesthood, political power, security, crafts, animal husbandry, agriculture, sexual behavior, family, and decision making. The myth probably was enacted in a festival or cult drama, one type of which was the journey drama, in which a deity traveled ritually from his or her home city to the city of another god, especially to Enki at Eridu, where great power was stored and could be obtained as a boon (Jacobsen, "Mesopotamian Religions," 464).

When Inanna visits him Enki provides a grand feast at which he becomes drunk and acts impulsively, eventually handing the *me* to the goddess. When, after a drunken sleep, he realizes what he has done, he sends his servant to get the *me* back, but Inanna has already departed, placing the *me* in her "boat of heaven," that is, the boat of Uruk-based An but also perhaps her ample vulva (Wolkstein and Kramer, 147). Enki's followers, aided by demons, chase the ship, but Inanna and her handmaiden Ninshubur hold off the pursuers with arguments and magic spells. Returning to Uruk with the *me*, the basis of what will be the well-being of the people of Uruk, a city that now perhaps achieves dominance over Eridu, Inanna holds a celebratory feast, and Enki accepts her new higher position among the gods.

Inanna and Utu

One day Inanna asks her twin brother, the sun god Utu (Shamash), son of the moon god Nanna, to go with her to earth (*kur*), where she will eat various plants and trees that will cause her to understand the mysteries of sex. Like Eve in the Garden of Eden, Inanna tastes the fruit and gains knowledge. In a related myth she descends to the *kur* (in this case *kur* is used in the sense of "underworld") to learn about good and evil. Returning from the *kur*, she falls asleep in a garden and is raped by a Sumerian man who then leaves her. Unable to find the man, the goddess sends plagues into Sumer in revenge. Later, apparently bathed by Enki in the *abzu*, she returns home purified.

Inanna and Dumuzi

After her adventures with Enki, Inanna becomes one of the four most important deities—truly a queen of heaven—but she has yet to fulfill her destiny as a goddess of erotic love and fertility. Utu, the sun god, who watches over growth on earth, reminds his twin sister that she is now ripe for love. Inanna has two suitors, the farmer Enkimdu and the shepherd Dumuzi. Inanna at first favors the farmer but finally decides on the shepherd, who woos her with Utu's enthusiastic support. Advised by her mother Ningal to "open [her] house" to Dumuzi, the goddess prepares her body for her husband-to-be. When she opens the door to him they are both overcome by passion. Inanna calls on her lover to fill her with his love:

> My vulva, the horn,
> The Boat of Heaven,
> Is full of eagerness like the young moon.
> My untilled land lies fallow.

And Dumuzi, the shepherd-farmer-king, obliges:

> I, Dumuzi, the King, will plow your vulva.
> (Wolkstein and Kramer, 37)

The love songs that follow are more explicit but in tone not unlike those to be found later in the biblical Song of Songs. All the senses play roles in the joyful private exploration of the physical that marks the sexual experience of Dumuzi and Inanna. But after the public consummation of the marriage, Dumuzi wishes to attend to his kingly duties and begs his wife to "set me free"; he no longer has time to make love "fifty times" (Wolkstein and Kramer, 150–53). This part of the myth is probably the earliest version of the universal story of conflict between love and duty.

The tradition of the sacred marriage is central to Mesopotamian culture, beginning probably at Inanna's city, Uruk, where, in a sacred ritual drama, the *en* enacted the role of Dumuzi as Amaushumgalana, the date palm god, bringing the harvest to Inanna, goddess of the storehouse-temple, who "opens [her] door" for him, signifying a marriage that would bring abundance to the city (Jacobsen, "Mesopotamian Religions," 464). The myth of the relationship between Inanna and Dumuzi, of course, underlies the sacred marriage ritual, even though some scholars have argued that Inanna was a goddess of erotic love, not a version of the mother goddess (Black and Green, 109). Certainly Inanna's marriage is a celebration of sexuality for its own sake as well as for fertility in Uruk. As noted above, Inanna's primary temple was at Uruk, where a king called Dumuzi, like Gilgamesh, appears on the king lists as an actual king of the city toward the end of the third millennium B.C.E.

Inanna's Descent to the Underworld

The myth of the hero's descent to the underworld is found in most cultures. The particular myth of Inanna's descent and Dumuzi's sacrifice adds the element of resurrection that links it in varying degrees to such stories as those of the Greek Persephone, the Egyptian Isis and Osiris, and the Christian Jesus. And these stories and others like them have in common the celebration of physical or spiritual fertility related to a ritual journey to the depths where shamanic powers are experienced or gained.

As queen of the above, Inanna, always in search of knowledge, longs to know the below of her sister Ereshkigal, the negative or opposite aspect of the ripe goddess of love. She understands life more fully than anyone, but she knows nothing of death or of the unhealthy, unfruitful sexuality of Ereshkigal. Before leaving for the underworld, Inanna instructs her faithful helper Ninshubur to arrange official mourning for her and to approach Enlil, Nanna, and Enki, in that order, for help if she should fail to return.

Inanna abandons her seven cities and seven temples, thus stripping herself in an official sense for the ritual journey to the dead. But she takes seven of the *me*, wearing them transformed into seven pieces of magnificent clothing and jewelry, and approaches the underworld in personal glory. She knocks on the great gates and demands admittance. When reasons are demanded, she first mentions her relationship to Ereshkigal and then claims to have come for the funeral of Gugalanna, the bull of heaven.

The bull of heaven was a figure traditionally linked to the generic great goddess, at least from the Neolithic period, and was important in Sumer as an animal representing the king of Uruk (in the present case, Dumuzi) as well as other kings and gods of Mesopotamia. He was also an astrological figure (Taurus), who disappeared in the winter in Sumer and returned in spring. The Gugalanna theme, then, supports the descent myth's association with agriculture and beneficial sacrifice (see Wolkstein and Kramer, 155ff.).

Neti, the guardian of the gates, informs the naked Ereshkigal of the grand visitor decked in the seven *me*. Furious at the intrusion of her opposite, of everything that she can never be—lover, mother—the queen of the underworld instructs her servant to allow Inanna through the seven locked gates of the underworld only if she gives up one of the seven objects (the *me* as ornaments and clothing) at each gate. When Inanna arrives at her sister's throne, then, she is as naked as her host and is thus effectively stripped of her great powers. The significance seems to be that powers that function in life—sexual, familial, political, and priestly powers, for example—are useless in death. Inanna, always in search of new roles, nevertheless tries to usurp her sister's throne and is condemned by the underworld Anunnaki (gods) to death for her efforts. She dies and is hung up on the wall like a piece of meat.

Back in Uruk, three days and nights have passed and the faithful Ninshubur follows her mistress's orders. The temples and cities go into deep mourning and Ninshubur approaches Inanna's paternal grandfather, Enlil, and then her father, Nanna, for help, but both refuse, blaming the goddess for her excessive pride in going to the underworld. But Enki, the wise shamanic god who from his home in the underground waters of the *abzu* has his ear to the underworld, agrees to help. He understands how important his granddaughter's existence is to the welfare of the living world (Wolkstein and Kramer, 159–60).

Enki creates two creatures from the mud under his fingernails. Apparently lacking sexuality or gender, these beings will not offend the infertile underworld, where Ereshkigal is screaming in pain as she gives negative birth, as it were, perhaps to the stillborn of the earth. To his two creatures Enki gives the plant of life and the water of life and instructs them to comfort the suffering Ereshkigal. In return the underworld queen will offer them gifts, which they will refuse, demanding instead the body of Inanna, which they will revive with the two sacred elements. Everything happens as foreseen by Enki, but the underworld Anunnaki demand a substitute for the revived Inanna. Although she has been reborn in the underworld, she must leave a part of herself there. As Samuel Noah Kramer suggests, from the world of consciousness above she must retain contact with the dark world of the unconscious below: "Inanna must not forget her neglected, abandoned older 'sister'—that part of herself that is Ereshkigal" (Wolkstein and Kramer, 161).

As Inanna leaves her sister's land, gathering up her clothing—her old *me* and power—she is accompanied by watchful demons who will ensure the payment of the sacrificial substitute. Entering her own world as once more the glorious queen of heaven, Inanna is greeted by Ninshubur, whose ragged clothes indicate her genuine mourning. When the demons claim the faithful servant as the sacrificial victim, Inanna refuses to give her up. Other faithful mourners—Inanna's two sons—are also spared, but when the great goddess and her underworld demons arrive at Uruk, a cheerful, well-dressed Dumuzi is acting as king, apparently unmindful of the loss of his once beloved wife. An enraged Inanna condemns him to the sacrifice. Terrified, Dumuzi begs his brother-in-law Utu for help, but even when he is turned by the sun god into a snake, he cannot escape. He, too, must experience the dark world of Inanna's other side, Ereshkigal, in order, as Kramer suggests, to become a "truly 'great' king" (163). Thus, Dumuzi is taken away, but his sister Gestinanna arranges to spend six months of the year in the underworld so that he can spend those months back in the world above.

Marduk, the Enuma Elish, and the Babylonian Creation

The Babylonian creation epic, the *Enuma Elish,* as we know it, is based on first-millennium B.C.E. tablet texts found at Assur, Nineveh,

Kish, and Uruk. In fact, the epic is primarily a celebration of the city of Babylon and its city god Marduk (*Bel,* "Lord"). It was recited at new year festivals in Babylon (and in Assyria at Nineveh, where Assur replaced Marduk as the protagonist). The composition of the epic probably coincides with and is intended to justify the rise of Marduk from his status as a minor Sumerian deity to chief of the Babylonian pantheon during the reign of Nebuchadnezzar I in the twelfth century B.C.E. (Leick, 52).

The rise of Marduk (and Assur) marks a significant change in the mythology of Mesopotamia, reflecting a movement from cultural principles centered on fertility and the balance of male and female roles to a much more patriarchal perspective such as the one that was emerging, for instance, among the Hebrews.

The *Enuma Elish* (the title translates as "when above") begins with a description of the beginning of time: "When the skies above were not yet named / Nor earth below pronounced by name, / Apsu, the first one, their begetter / And maker [*mummu*] Tiamat, who bore them all, / Had mixed their waters together" (Dalley, 233). Out of this mixture of sweet (Apsu) and salt water (Tiamat) came the gods—first the ill-defined Lahmu and Lahamu ("hairy ones"), then Anshar and Kishar, who produced Anu (the Sumerian An). Ea (Nudimmud, Sumerian Enki) was born in Anu's image. The new beings made so much noise that Apsu became irritated; encouraged by his vizier Mummu, he decided to get rid of them to restore peace and quiet. Tiamat, however, could not bear to harm her offspring. In this she resembles the Greek primal mother goddesses who try to protect their offspring against their child-destroying father-god mates. It was Ea who, like Zeus in Greek mythology, came to the rescue of the new gods. Using his inborn shamanic or magical powers, he cast a spell over Apsu, sending him to sleep forever as the underground waters, the *apsu* (Sumerian *abzu*), where, with his wife, Damkina (Sumerian Damgalnuna), he produced the great Marduk. Marduk was a huge, powerful god with four heads who irritated Tiamat by causing great waves and noise, thus establishing his identity as a storm god. When Anu created the winds, they added to Tiamat's noise, and Tiamat, assisted and encouraged by certain other gods, began to form an army of monsters led by her son Qingu (Kingu) to do away with Marduk and the noise. Worried about what Tiamat might do to them, the gods called on Anu and Ea for help, but they realized their powerlessness against Tiamat and refused. Ea advised Marduk to take up their cause, and he agreed, but with the stipulation that the gods recognize him as their new king. It was he who from now on would decide destinies.

Marduk approached the wild and angry Tiamat as a storm god and filled her grotesque and open mouth with wind so that she could not devour him, and then he pierced her bloated belly with an arrow and threw her dead body to the ground. When the monster-mother's army tried to escape, Marduk captured them and took the tablets of destiny away from Qingu. Now Marduk was ready to create the world.

The creation myths express the cultures' sense of themselves, their essential identities. For several millennia Mesopotamia had generally accepted the old Sumerian creation story in which the female aspect is positive and important, basic to the fertility and irrigation principles so necessary for the agricultural practices of the Sumerians. But now the storm god Marduk, the all-dominant male, would create a world out of the dead body of the defeated feminine power that had been Tiamat. In the context of the new Babylonian national priorities— including a determination to confront threats to their hegemony by people of the so-called Sea Land in the old Sumerian territory south of them—his victory and creation signify strong hierarchical power and male reason as opposed to a kind of irrational, watery chaos represented by the female Tiamat and the old ways (Frymer-Kensky, "Enuma Elish," 124–26).

Marduk creates the world by crushing Tiamat and dividing her dead body into two parts. Half of the body he sets up as the sky, the other half as the earth. Her head becomes a mountain, her eyes the Tigris and Euphrates Rivers. Her breasts he turns into hills, her nostrils reservoirs. Besides this, Marduk creates the planets and stars, establishes the separation of waters, and generally gets the world operating properly. Finally, he establishes the city of Babylon as a temple home for all of the gods, thus achieving cultural and national unity and hegemony. Marduk instructs Ea to make use of the dead Qingu's blood to create humans, who would do the work that otherwise the gods would have to do, and he prescribes functions for each of the gods. In short, he brings order to what the Babylonians had seen as the chaotic religious and social system of the past. So it is that

the gods build the temple of Marduk as the primary temple of Babylon and celebrate him there as the supreme deity.

Mesopotamian Heroes and Their Myths

As in much of the world, a tradition developed in ancient Mesopotamia in which historical figures were mythologized into heroes
possessing supernatural origins and superhuman powers. Etana, a
Sumerian shepherd-king of Kish, sought the plant of life and ascended to heaven. Sargon of Akkad, who conquered Sumer in the
third millennium, was said to have been born of a humble mother and
a mysteriously unknown father. Like Moses, Siegfried, and many
other heroes after him, he was placed in a basket as a child, abandoned in the river (in this case the Euphrates), and found and
brought up by a person of the menial class. The goddess Ishtar supported him, however, and he became king and then "living god" of
Akkad (Campbell, *Hero*, 321). At least three kings of Uruk were
mythologized as heroes in epic-type literature written down about
2100 B.C.E. from earlier oral versions. These kings had lived before
2600 B.C.E. First there was Enmerkar, who was said to have been
closely related to Utu and Inanna, his protector, and to have invented
writing. Then there was Lugalbanda, whose wife was said to have
been the mother of Dumuzi and Gilgamesh. This goddess, Ninsun,
was "mistress of the cows," a designation that ties her to the most ancient of Middle Eastern goddesses. Finally, there was the greatest of
Mesopotamian heroes, Gilgamesh himself.

Enmerkar and Enshukeshdanna

In a text from the Ur III period, Enshukeshdanna, lord of Aratta,
challenges his rival, Enmerkar, king of Uruk, by claiming to be the
true husband of the goddess Inanna. As Inanna is particularly the patroness of Uruk and the ritual "bride" of its king, Enmerkar takes the
challenge seriously and reacts with great anger, condemning Enshukeshdanna and asserting his right to Inanna. The king of Aratta
sends a magician to Eres, a town near Uruk, where he dries up the

milk of the sacred stables. The shepherds in the area beg the god Utu for help, and suddenly Sagburru, a wise crone from Eres, comes on the scene and challenges the sorcerer of Aratta to a contest involving the transformation of objects. Both magicians throw metal objects into the river. The man's turns into a carp, the woman's into an eagle that eats the carp. Then the man's ewe and lamb are eaten by the woman's wolf, and so it goes until the man gives in and the old woman throws him to his death in the river. Upon hearing the news, Enshukeshdanna agrees that Enmerkar is the true bridegroom of Inanna (Leick, 50; Kerrigan, Lothian, and Vitebsky, 66–68).

Enmerkar and the Lord of Aratta

Another story about the same rivalry dates from the Old Babylonian period.

King Enmerkar of Uruk decides that the people of Aratta should come to Uruk with valuables and building materials so as to build temples for him there and in Eridu. Inanna, always Uruk's patroness, agrees to help and advises the king to send a messenger to Aratta demanding the materials in question. When the lord of Aratta refuses, claiming his own closeness to Inanna, the messenger reminds him of Enmerkar's even closer relationship and of Inanna's claim that Aratta would have to submit to Uruk. The king agrees to submit to Enmerkar if the latter will agree to a contest. Enmerkar agrees, as his success will prove Inanna's loyalty to him. In the midst of completing several impossible tasks, Enmerkar sends a herald with a written message to Aratta. Thus he invents writing. In the message he agrees to a combat between dogs from each city, again demands the materials for temple building and decoration, and threatens the destruction of Aratta should the conditions of the demand not be met. Although much of the text is lost, it seems likely that Enmerkar's dog wins the fight, as the story ends with the people of Aratta bringing the requested materials to Uruk (Leick, 51–52).

Lugalbanda in the Mountains

Lugalbanda is with his king, Enmerkar, in the mountains on the way to a war with the lord of Aratta in the east. Suddenly he loses his ability to move, and his comrades are forced to leave him alone with some food and some weapons until they can retrieve him on their way home. The hero prays to Utu, Inanna, and Nanna, the paralysis leaves him, and good demons find him the plant and water of life, which he eats and drinks. Now full of energy, he hunts for more food and captures several wild animals. In his sleep he is told to sacrifice the animals and to offer the hearts to Utu and the blood to the mountain serpents. Lugalbanda does as he is instructed and then prepares a feast to which he invites An, Enlil, and Ninhursaga. As evening approaches, the astral deities to whom he has prayed and for whom he has made special altars reveal themselves in the night sky and chase away any evil powers (Leick, 111).

Gilgamesh

Easily the most famous of Mesopotamian heroes is Gilgamesh. The mythologizing of this Early Dynastic period Sumerian king of Unug (Uruk) had already begun by about 2400 B.C.E., when Gilgamesh, or Bilgamesh, was worshiped at several Sumerian sites. It is even possible that he was deified during his lifetime (c. 2650 B.C.E.), because of his building of the walls of Uruk and his defense of Uruk against the rival city of Kish. By the Ur III period he had become lord of the underworld, a role that led in later years to a complex burial cult. Gilgamesh was always closely associated with the sun god Utu (Shamash) and was often identified with Dumuzi, also a deified king of Uruk. As noted above, it was said that his mother was the goddess Ninsun and his father the deified hero Lugalbanda. Ur III and Isin kings (c. 2100–1900) especially considered Gilgamesh their ancestor and used that connection to justify their rule. It is usually suggested that the Sumerian myths of Gilgamesh were developed during this period, perhaps including a hero birth story that, however, does not appear in any text until classical times (Black and Green, 91). In that story, which has archetypal relatives in those of Etana, Sargon, Moses, and even Jesus, a king's daughter becomes pregnant, and a court magus asserts that the child will take the king's throne. This causes the king to have the child thrown from a tower. The child is saved in midfall by a flying eagle and is adopted and raised by an orchard worker. Later, of course, he becomes king.

There are five written stories of Gilgamesh dating from the Sumerian period, and they do not seem to have been combined in anything like the epic form of the tale that was composed later in Babylon.

"Gilgamesh and Agga" (or "The Man of Sumer") tells how King Gilgamesh of Uruk, besieged behind his walls by his enemy, Agga of Kish, used a distracting trick and was able to capture his enemy before generously pardoning him.

"Gilgamesh and the Land of the Living" (or "Gilgamesh and Huwawa" or "Gilgamesh and the Cedar Forest") exists in many forms and plays a role in the Babylonian epic as well. Hating the sight of death and wishing to achieve fame and immortality, Gilgamesh, with his follower Enkidu and with guidance from the sun god Utu, sets out to fight Huwawa, the monstrous caretaker of the Cedar Forest sacred to the great god Enlil. When they get there Enkidu is fearful, but Gilgamesh braves the powerful rays with which the monster plagues them, and cuts down trees so as to be able to capture him. After the capture Huwawa pleads for his life, but the angry Enkidu cuts off his head. For this act the heroes are cursed by Enlil.

"Gilgamesh and the Bull of Heaven," which exists only in fragments, tells how Gilgamesh disdainfully refused the advances of the beautiful Inanna and how he killed the bull of heaven sent by the goddess to avenge the insult to her.

"Gilgamesh, Enkidu, and the Netherworld" (or "Gilgamesh and the *Huluppu* Tree") does not follow logically from the bull of heaven story, as it reveals a much different relationship between the hero and Inanna. It is from the beginning of or introduction to this myth that the Sumerian creation story discussed earlier can be derived. After the creation, Inanna takes a windswept *huluppu* tree from the riverbank and plants it in her temple at Uruk. Her plan is to make furniture from it when it is full-grown, but when that time comes she finds that her plans are foiled by the inhabitants of the tree, the powerful and dangerous *anzu* bird, the despondent maiden Lilit (Lilith), and a mean serpent. Even Inanna's brother Utu cannot help her dislodge the three demonic creatures, but Gilgamesh can. He successfully kills the serpent, scaring away the other demons, and the tree is cut down and used for Inanna's sacred furniture. Inanna uses part of the wood to make two mysterious objects called the *pukku* and the *mukku*,

which somehow fall into the netherworld. When Enkidu offers to retrieve them, Gilgamesh cautions his friend and servant about the
taboos of the underworld and allows him to go. Because Enkidu fails
to follow the instructions he is not able to return to the world above.
Even Enlil and Enki are unable to help the hero retrieve his friend,
but the shamanic Enki instructs Utu to burn a hole in the ground, by
way of which Enkidu's ghost emerges and tells Gilgamesh about existence in the underworld.

"The Death of Gilgamesh" is a mere fragment in which Gilgamesh
expresses resentment about his death. Several scholars have suggested
that it might really be the story of Enkidu's death (Leick, 71; Black
and Green, 89).

We know Gilgamesh best through what is probably the earliest example of an epic poem. The so-called epic of Gilgamesh certainly had
oral roots, but it was first expressed in written (Akkadian) form in the
Old Babylonian period of the early second millennium B.C.E. A more
complete version was written later, in the Middle Babylonian period,
supposedly by one Sin-leqe-unnini, and there are Neo-Babylonian,
Neo-Assyrian, Hittite, and other versions. The epic had gained popularity in much of the Middle East by the middle of the second millennium B.C.E. It was apparently the Middle Babylonian version that was
the basis for most of the Ninevite recension, the approximately 1,500-
line epic in twelve tablets discovered in the Assyrian Library of Assurbanipal at Nineveh dating from the seventh century B.C.E.

Unlike the Gilgamesh of the Sumerian fragments, the hero of the
Babylonian Gilgamesh epic is distinctly human rather than divine. In
fact, if there is an underlying theme to the whole epic, it is Gilgamesh's
discovery of his mortality in his passage from arrogance to humility in
a quest for immortality. William Moran suggests that Gilgamesh's
passage reflects the "ideological developments of the period that to
some extent demythologized kingship and rejected the divinity that
kings had been claiming for five centuries or so." Furthermore, the epic
emphasizes the difference between humans and deities in general,
based in the fact that even a hero, a goddess's son, "must perform the
very human and undivine act of dying" (Moran, 559).

The epic opens with what is essentially a hymn to the great King
Gilgamesh of Uruk, builder of city walls, writer of his many experiences

and journeys on tablets, son of Ninsun. In a sense this is a hymn of praise and even human arrogance that serves as the preface for the rites of passage from ignorance to knowledge that will follow. The seed of disillusionment, the existence of a significant flaw, makes itself evident even within the first tablet, when we learn that the king has tyrannized his people by demanding conjugal rights to brides. When the people complain to Anu, the god instructs Aruru, the mother goddess, to create a being who can balance Gilgamesh's power. The new creation is the hairy, bestial Enkidu, who eats grass and frees animals trapped by huntsmen. When the existence of Enkidu is reported to Gilgamesh he follows the advice of the huntsmen and sends out the beautiful prostitute Samhat to tame him. It should be remembered that prostitutes were sacred to Ishtar (Inanna). The tactic works. Enkidu and Samhat make love for six days and seven nights until Enkidu has been humanized, told about Gilgamesh, and deprived of some of his purely animal nature. The reader here can hardly avoid a fleeting vision of the story of Samson and Delilah.

Back in Uruk Gilgamesh dreams of Enkidu and then recurrently of heavy objects that have come from the sky, objects to which he feels sexually attracted. Gilgamesh's mother, Ninsun, interprets the dreams for her son, explaining that they are about a man who will become his companion and closest friend. Many critics have suggested a homosexual aspect to the Gilgamesh-Enkidu relationship, as indicated first by these dreams and then by later events (Leick, 73; Moran, 558).

In Tablet 2 the love of Gilgamesh and Enkidu is consummated, as it were, in a manly wrestling match that is barely won by the king, but Enkidu's courage and power impress Gilgamesh and the two become companions. The next three tablets concern the adventures of the two heroes in the Cedar Forest of Enlil, guarded by Humbaba (the Sumerian Huwawa). There, presumably, they kill the monster, as indicated in other versions of the story.

What follows, in Tablet 6, is the surprising story of Gilgamesh's refusal of Ishtar (Sumerian Inanna), based on the Sumerian story mentioned above. The heroes are back in Uruk, and the newly cleansed and adorned king is approached by Ishtar with a proposition of love and marriage and fertility for himself, his city, and its fields and animals. Gilgamesh rejects the offer outright, pointing to the tragic ends

of so many of the goddess's former lovers. Furious, Ishtar has Anu
send the bull of heaven to attack the heroes. After the beast kills hun-
dreds of people—perhaps representing a plague—the heroes succeed
in killing him. Gilgamesh further insults his divine enemy by flinging
a thigh of the beast at her.

Gilgamesh's rejection of Ishtar is difficult to understand, given the
fact that she was the city goddess of Uruk and that the sacred marriage of king and goddess had been a foundation of Mesopotamian
culture at least since the Old Sumerian period. There is the possibility
that the incident somehow reflects the demythologizing of divine
kings as well as a movement away from the strong goddess aspect of
religion and culture to the kind of patriarchy revealed also in the
Enuma Elish. But this interpretation is somewhat undermined by the
existence of the earlier Sumerian version of the story. It is possible
that the reaction of Gilgamesh is simply demanded by his particular
character or persona, one that prefers the company of Enkidu to that
of Ishtar.

In Tablet 7 Enkidu dreams that Anu, Ea, and Shamash have decided that for the killing of Humbaba and the bull of heaven either he
or Gilgamesh must pay with his life. Enkidu fades into sickness; in
Tablet 8 he dies and is lamented by the heartbroken Gilgamesh.

Tablet 9 concerns Gilgamesh's fear of death and his danger-filled
journey in what is, in effect, a kind of archetypal underworld. He
must convince the horrible scorpion people to let him pass through a
long, dark tunnel. And there is the relationship with the beautiful
alewife Siduri in her jeweled garden. Siduri will have "sisters" in the
Odyssey's Calypso and Circe and the *Aeneid*'s Dido, women who,
through love, would prevent the patriarchal hero from completing his
mission. Like Ishtar, Siduri is a comfortable alternative that must be
overcome. Still, like Circe in the *Odyssey,* she finally helps the hero on
his way with advice on how to proceed, and in Tablet 10 Gilgamesh is
ferried across the waters of death by the ferryman Urshanabi. On the
other side he finds the ancient flood hero Utnapishtim (Ziusudra in
an older Sumerian flood myth), who reminds his visitor that only the
gods determine life and death.

Tablet 11 contains the flood myth, which is remarkably similar to
the one found in Genesis in the Bible. Gilgamesh asks Utnapishtim

to explain how he has attained eternal life, and the old man answers by reciting the story of the flood.

Utnapishtim and his wife had lived in Shuruppak. Ea had come to him there to announce that a flood was about to destroy humanity. He and his family would be spared only if they built a boat, for which the gods provided the measurements. When the boat was finished, Utnapishtim filled it with valuables, his own family, and representatives of all the species. Then came the most terrible of storms and a deluge that destroyed the earth. After seven days the storm died down and the ship landed on Mount Nisir. After another week a dove was released to find land, but it returned unsuccessful to the ship. The same thing happened when a swallow was released, but when a released raven did not come back Utnapishtim realized that he had been saved. He made offerings of thanks to the gods; the mother goddess, in great distress, promised always to remember him. After much discussion Enlil granted Utnapishtim eternal life.

Gilgamesh, too, longs for eternal life, but Utnapishtim is skeptical of his ability to obtain it. As a test, he challenges the hero to stay awake for six days and seven nights. Gilgamesh, exhausted, immediately falls asleep, and the flood hero's wife bakes a loaf of bread for each day he remains in that state. When Gilgamesh wakes up he sees the now moldy bread and realizes the point of Utnapishtim's challenge. He is human, with human frailties. Eternal life is beyond his powers. Before he leaves, Utnapishtim, at the urging of his wife, tells Gilgamesh about a plant under the water that can provide youth. On his way home with Urshanabi the hero dives for the plant and retrieves it. But once again, being merely human, he falls asleep, and a serpent steals the plant. So it is that serpents slough off old skin and become new again.

Gilgamesh weeps in despair, but he and Urshanabi, abandoning the latter's boat, make their way to Uruk. There Gilgamesh proudly asks the ferryman to inspect his great wall and his fine city. In a sense, the hero accepts his humanity.

Tablet 12 is a late addition to the epic, present only in the Ninevite recension. It is a retelling of "Gilgamesh, Enkidu, and the Netherworld," in which the shade of Enkidu tells Gilgamesh about the underworld and the necessity of burying the dead. (Black and Green, 89–91; Leick, 68–77; Moran, 557–60; Dalley, 39–49).

7

◈

The Mythology of Egypt

Egyptian mythology is dominated by the theme of a sacred kingship and the related theme of death and the afterlife, often in relation to the role of the Nile in a cyclical process by which the land dies and is reborn. Underlying these themes is a tension between light and darkness—between the supreme solar deity, usually Re (Ra), and the god of earth, fertility, and the underworld, Osiris. The Egyptians, as revealed in their myths, their rituals, their funerary writings, and their symbolic art and architecture, were preoccupied—more philosophically than the Mesopotamians, for instance—with questions of the nature of the universe and the relation of humans to the unknown. Their deities and their myths, highly symbolic vehicles for complex theologies, varied considerably in particulars according to the era and the cult center. But different centers assimilated each other's versions of deities and generally participated in what was a constant revisiting and revision of myths from very ancient times. The various local traditions had in common the central themes mentioned above and the highly philosophical and symbolic treatment of them.

As in the case of other prehistoric cultures in the Middle East and elsewhere, the predynastic mythology of Egypt can only be surmised by way of archeological remains. It is likely, as indicated in burial sites, where bodies are buried in a fetal position with the head south and facing west, that there was a belief in the afterlife. Leonard Lesko suggests the possibility of a sun god cult involving death and the setting sun or an early stage of the Osiris-type cult associated with a western necropolis (Lesko, "Egyptian Religion," 39). R. T. Rundle Clark and others assume the existence of a mother goddess cult such as the one we find indicated in Çatal Hüyük and other ancient sites (Clark, 28). This position is supported by the persistence among the Egyptian people over the centuries of the goddess cult as represented by Hathor, Neith, Maat, Ejo, and Isis, among others, at various ancient cult sites along the Nile.

We are on much surer ground with Egyptian mythology when we come to the Early Dynastic period—specifically the First and Second Dynasties, beginning perhaps as early as 3100 B.C.E. During these dynastic periods, hieroglyphic writing was developed, and Upper and Lower Egypt were unified with a capital at Memphis under the kingship of Narmer or Aha, known in combination as Menes. This was the first great nation-state of history, and its kingship seems already to have been justified by a sacred association of the king with the god Horus, represented by the emblematic falcon on one side of the slate palette—the so-called Narmer Palette—of the first monarch and the bull of kingly power on the other (Lesko, "Egyptian Religion," 39; Campbell, *Oriental*, 51ff.). The fact that kings of the Second Dynasty associated themselves in their titles with Horus and Seth and then in the south simply with Seth indicates a possible early development of the Osiris cult with its antithesis between Horus and Seth, a mythological antithesis that spoke to the historical split at the end of the Second Dynasty between the kingdoms of Upper and Lower Egypt.

The Pantheons

It is during the Old Kingdom (Third through Sixth Dynasties, c. 2700–2190) that an Egyptian pantheon begins to take form in the context of developed theologies. Over the centuries theologies and their particular versions of the pantheon would develop at several major cult centers. The generally dominant theology was that formulated by the priests at Heliopolis, north of present-day Cairo. But important interpretations came from Memphis, also in the Cairo area, from Herakleopolis and Hermopolis and, briefly, Akhetaton (Amarna) further south, as well as from the major sites in deep Upper Egypt: Thebes (modern Luxor and Karnak), Abydos, Dendera, Esna, and Edfu.

The High God

The high god of Egypt was a creator god, usually associated with the sun. In Memphis, the first capital, he probably began as the falcon-headed sky and sun god Horus, the source of earthly kingship. Soon, however, he emerged in the highly complex Memphite theology as Ptah, the god of the primeval mound (Tatenen), who created by thinking things "in his heart" and then naming them with speech. His wife was the lioness goddess Sekhmet. Ptah's human form was that of a man in a cloak holding a scepter. Later he was identified with the pantheon of Khemenu, or Hermopolis. The Hermopolitan pantheon, known as the Ogdoad or "the eight," was made up of four couples representing primordial chaotic forces. Amun (Amon) and Amaunet were forces of the invisible, Huh (Heh) and Hauhet (Hehet) were forces of infinity, Kuk (Kek) and Kauhet (Keket) were forces of darkness, and Nun and Naunet were the primal waters. In Memphis, Ptah was equated for a time with Nun and Naunet, out of whom was said to have come the creator god Atum (Lesko, "Ptah").

In the theology of Heliopolis, Atum was "the whole one," the creator who contained male and female. He was the head and founder of the Ennead, "the nine." Atum produced Shu and Tefnut (air and moisture), the progenitors of Geb and Nut (earth and sky), in turn the parents of Osiris and Seth and their sister wives Isis and Neph-thys. Horus as the son of Osiris and Isis was an added, tenth member of the Ennead.

During the Old Kingdom Fifth Dynasty, Atum was displaced by or assimilated with the ancient sun god Re (Pre, Ra), the high god now becoming simply Re or Atum-Re or Re-Atum. As the center of the sun cult in later times, Re was Re-Harakhte (meaning "Re-Horus of the Great Horizon"), the personification of the noonday sun, and was usually depicted as a human with the head of a hawk surmounted by a sun disk. The rising sun was Re as Khepri, the scarab. The

evening sun was Re-Atum. Re assimilated the sacred king cult of Horus as indicated by Horus's title in the so-called Pyramid Texts of the
Fifth Dynasty as "son of Re." Horus's mother in this configuration
was Re's consort, the great cow goddess Hathor, a personification of
the Ennead itself (Lesko, "Atum"; Lesko, "Egyptian Religion,"
39–40; Lesko, "Re"). The Pyramid Texts reveal a further accommodation of the solar and sacred kingship cults by describing the king as
a god who guards Re in his daily trip across the sky in his solar bark.

During the Middle Kingdom (2050–1756 B.C.E.) under the new
rulers based in Thebes, an assimilation of gods took place that included the still-powerful Re. The Theban war god Montu merged
with Amun, the Hermopolitan primal force of the invisible, and with
the fertility god of the Coptos, the ithyphallic Min. To this mixture
Re was added and Amun-Re came to the fore, especially at the Theban cult center of Karnak, as the sun god and king of gods. Represented with a ram's head, Amun-Re was accompanied by his consort,
the mother goddess Mut. Their son was the moon god Khonsu.

Still another expression of the high creator god was Khnum at
Esna, south of Thebes. Khnum, depicted with the head of a ram, created the primal world egg at his potter's wheel. He was one of the
earliest of the *deus faber* (craftsman god) creators, although in some
stories Ptah, too, was such a creator, molding beings out of metal
(Bently, 114, 176).

Finally, during the Amarna period (c. 1353–1327 B.C.E.) of the
pharaoh Amenhotep IV, who disassociated himself from Amun-Re
and renamed himself Akhenaton (Ikhnaton), there was the god Aton
(Aten), represented as a sun disk, the rays of which reach down to the
earth as hands. Although it has been fashionable over the centuries to
consider Aton a sole god and to claim Akhenaton as the founder of
monotheism, it seems more likely that Aton was a manifestation of
Re and was one among several gods worshiped at the time
(Wasilewska, 95–96). Still, it is true that the pharaoh greatly favored
the god from whose name he took *his* new name and the name of his
new capital, Akhetaton (Amarna). The son of Akhenaton and Nefertiti, Tutankhaton (c. 1348–1339 B.C.E.), better known as "King Tut,"
changed his name to Tutankhamun to reflect a restoration of the
Amun cult.

The Great Goddess

Egyptian mythology has many versions of the great mother goddess found in cultures throughout the Middle East and other parts of the ancient world. It seems likely that the mother goddess tradition existed as a powerful force in prehistoric Egypt (Clark, 87). One of the earliest historical forms is that of the cow goddess, Hathor. Other expressions of the cow goddess existed, as we have seen, at least from the Neolithic period and were prevalent among the goddesses of Mesopotamia, who were contemporaries of Hathor. Both sides of the Narmer Palette of the Old Kingdom First Dynasty of Memphis are presided over by heads of Hathor as a cow—four heads in all, representing the four directions, the four corners of the sky, the "Hathor of the horizon" (Campbell, *Oriental*, 52–53). Hathor was the all-enveloping sky goddess who, often with the sun within her horns, was the daughter of Re. As a cow, she suckled the baby Horus, and her name can be translated as "house of Horus." As such, she is, as noted earlier, the personification of the whole pantheon or Ennead of Heliopolis as well as of *maat*, meaning "truth" or "proper order" (Campbell, *Oriental*, 54), a concept not unlike the Mesopotamian *me*. She was, as we learn from the Coffin Texts of the late third millennium B.C.E., also the "Eye of Horus" or Re, the Kali-like destroyer goddess, the sun that burns the desert.

Hathor's cult center was in the south at Dendera. She was the "eye" in the north also, taking the form of the guardian cobra goddess Wadjet (Wedjat), whose symbol was placed on the forehead of pharaohs and who sometimes appeared as a pair—Ejo (north) and Nekhabit the vulture (south).

An important form of the great goddess in the delta was Neith, "the oldest goddess, the Mother of the Gods" (Clark 206). Neith was said to have emerged from Nun, the primal waters, and to have been a creatrix of gods and humans and to have been sought out by the gods for important advice.

The goddess was also Sekhmet, the lioness wife of Ptah who was both an annihilator and a savior of humankind, and Mut, the wife of Amun-Re.

In the creation myth of Heliopolis several goddesses play important roles. Tefnut (Tefenet) is a personification of moisture, who mated with Shu (air) and gave birth to sky as the goddess Nut, who mated with her brother earth, as Geb. From the union of Geb and Nut came, among others, the most popular of Egyptian goddesses, Isis, the mother of Horus, whose story is so central to that of her brother-husband, the resurrection god Osiris, and around whom a cult developed that lasted well into Roman times. Isis was her husband's queen in the underworld and the theological basis for the role of the queen on earth. She was the mother of Horus and the "throne" (*isis*) of Osiris. It can be said that she was a version of the great goddess as Hathor. Like Hathor, she not only had death and rebirth associations but was the protectress of children and the goddess of childbirth. On her head the great cow horns of Hathor supported the solar disk (Lesko, "Isis").

The Dying God

Osiris, the first son of Nut (sky) and Geb (earth), was perhaps the most important of Egyptian gods. He stands at the very center of the most characteristic themes of ancient Egyptian mythology and culture. As the first mythical king of Egypt—literally a god-king—and as the source (the father) of the god-king Horus, he was the theological basis for the eternal and sacred kingship. The pharaoh died as Osiris and was resurrected as his son Horus. As the dying god who was resurrected and who became king of the underworld and was not only the dying pharaoh but eventually, as we are told in the Coffin Texts and the *Book of Going Forth by Day* (the *Book of the Dead*), any dying human, he was the basis for the Egyptian practice of mummification and afterlife belief in general. Furthermore, Osiris's life, death, and resurrection are metaphors for the central life-giving phenomenon in Egypt, the annual death and resurrection of the land flooded by the Nile. And as the resurrection god, who was usually depicted as a mummy, sometimes in an ithyphallic state, Osiris was, quite logically, a fertility god represented by the sprouting of crops after the flood. The fertility aspect was emphasized by the association of Osiris at Memphis with the Apis bull, an association that developed in the Ptolemaic and Roman periods into the cult of Serapis, a combination of Osiris and Apis. Osiris was said to have been born at Busiris and to have died at Abydos, his principal cult center (Lesko, "Osiris").

Closely associated with Osiris is the jackal- or dog-headed Anubis (Anpu), who in his earliest form devoured the dead. Later, as funerary practices developed, he became the embalmer—especially of the dead Osiris—and the protector of graves. He was sometimes depicted lying on the chest containing the inner organs of the deceased. Anubis was the son of Osiris by Osiris's sister Nephthys. He served Osiris in the underworld as a judge of the dead, and he became a Hermes-like conductor of souls in the mystery cult of Isis in Roman times (van Voss, 330–31).

Trickster Gods

In a very general sense the gods Seth and Thoth might be understood as negative and positive aspects of the archetypal trickster god. Seth, like so many tricksters, was amoral and was driven by Iago-like pure evil, jealousy, and greed. Like other sometimes reprehensible tricksters—Loki in Scandinavia, Ananse in Africa, Coyote in North America, for instance—he was extremely clever and could play positive roles as well. Early in the Old Kingdom, as we have seen, he was the patron of certain dynasties. And in his positive aspect, again like several trickster gods, he assisted the high god/creator. He was sometimes shown as a guardian of Re's sun bark, using his magic spells to defend it against the serpent Apopis (Apep). Depicted with floppy ears and an erect and divided tail, he was, however, more usually a negative deity, standing in the way especially of the "good" gods, Osiris and his son Horus. Seth's wife was his sister Nephthys, who helped Isis to revive Osiris. Theologically speaking, Seth performed the necessary role of death and destruction in the overall process of life. It was he who was responsible for the death of Osiris and for the loss of one of Horus's eyes—the moon—which was retrieved by Thoth (Lesko, "Seth"; Clark, 224).

Thoth was the moon god as well as the god of wisdom. In Hermopolis, his theological home, he gave the dead who were initiated into his secrets passage to the sky. His is the realm of the mysteries, magic, and arcane knowledge, such as that contained in the *Book of Going Forth by Day*. It was he who invented hieroglyphs and writing. In Hermopolis he might sometimes have been seen as a creator god

(Lesko, "Thoth," 493). For some, Thoth was the son of Re, Re in this case being the sun, the right eye of Horus, whose moon eye had been ripped out by Seth. His consort was Maat, the personification of divine order and justice. Thoth's head was that of a baboon or an ibis. As a funerary god, like Anubis, he weighed the hearts of the deceased. He was, as Joseph Campbell has written, "master of the word and of the magic of resurrection" (*Oriental*, 86–87). Early in the New Kingdom, certain pharaohs chose the name Thothmose (Thutmose) to associate themselves with this great and mysterious god (Lesko, "Thoth," 493). This was a family that considered itself particularly close to divinity. When Hatshepsut, the wife of Thothmose II, usurped the throne on her husband's death, she justified her action by claiming a particularly divine birth. She was the female version of Horus, conceived when Amun-Re took the form of her earthly father, Thothmose I, and had relations with Hatshepsut's mother, Ahmose (Lesko, "Egyptian Religion," 42).

Egyptian Cosmic Myths

The Heliopolitan Creation and Cosmology

As contained primarily in the Pyramid Texts originating in Heliopolis beginning in about 2350 B.C.E., the Heliopolitan cosmogony is generally considered to be the most orthodox. Like all versions of the Egyptian creation, it starts from the concept of the primeval waters— in some areas, especially Hermopolis, personified as Nun, the father of gods. Nun contained the essential energy of the dark and formless chaos out of which creation emerged. This creation, as R. T. Rundle Clark suggests, signified four aspects of existence: "light, life, land, and consciousness" (Clark, 36). From the primeval waters arose the god Atum—later Atum-Re—as the primeval mound, symbolized by the pyramids themselves and perhaps having its source in the creative mounds left annually by the receding floodwaters of the Nile. Atum-Re was Heliopolis itself and also the light of the rising sun and the embodiment of the conscious Word or Logos, the essence of life. In the somewhat later (c. 2000 B.C.E.) *Book of Going Forth by Day*, the emerging god or "becoming one," the visible form of the invisible

Atum, was Khepri, the scarab, the symbol of the rebirth of the sun that looked down from the sky as the god Re.

Like so many first gods in other cultures, Atum required the existence of others to render himself significant. As the all encompassing "great he-she," he had no mate but his hand—later known as the hand goddess Iusas. With that hand he masturbated "that he might obtain the pleasure of emission," and in so doing he produced the brother and sister Shu and Tefnut, air and moisture—life and order in the later Coffin Texts. In one Pyramid Texts version, Atum spit Shu and Tefnut into existence. This version, conveying the idea of creation from the mouth, suggests the sense expressed in the Memphite creation, in which Ptah created by thinking and naming "by word of mouth."

Shu and Tefnut, who were also associated with the sun and moon, gave birth to the male god Geb (earth) and the female Nut (sky). Geb and Nut at first lay together as one being but were separated by their perhaps jealous father, Shu, who, as air, provided space between earth and sky where other beings could be created. The theme of the separation of primordial parents to provide room for creation is a common one in world mythology. While no narrative exists for this Egyptian version of the myth, the story is depicted in many paintings, in which Geb is shown, sometimes with an erect penis, lying on his back as his sister-wife arches over him, often held up by her father Shu.

Separated from Geb, Nut could give birth to the stars, who rose to her. Each day she swallowed these children so as to protect them until they could be reborn at night. Together Geb and Nut produced Osiris and Seth and their sisters Isis and Nephthys, the principles, with the god Horus—the son of Isis and Osiris—of what the Egyptians saw as the primary drama of earthly existence, that of life, death, and rebirth.

The Hermopolitan Creation

In the Middle Egyptian city of Hermopolis (Khemenu), an emphasis was placed on the great abyss of nothingness out of which creation came. This primordial chaos, the primeval waters or abyss, was made up of the four pairs that together were the Hermopolitan pantheon of eight, the Ogdoad. Huh and Hauhet, Nun and Naunet, Amun and

Amaunet, and Kuk and Kauhet—"the infinity, the nothingness, the nowhere and the dark"—are the negative or undifferentiated foundation for the primeval egg that was the immediate source of creation. In some tellings of the story it was the god Thoth in his ibis form who laid the primeval egg on the primeval mound formed by the Ogdoad. Another story held that it was the primeval goose, the "great cackler," who laid the egg. The egg was said to contain the sun god, who in another Hermopolitan myth was born as a divine child from a lotus. It was this god who would create the world (Wasilewska, 60ff.; Clark, 54ff.).

The Memphite Creation

Our source for the ancient creation myth of Memphis is a late text copied down from a much earlier text during the reign of the Nubian pharaoh Shabago during the Twenty-fifth Dynasty (c. 700 B.C.E.). In this document, the Memphite priests have asserted the dominance of their high god, Ptah, over the gods of Heliopolis and Hermopolis. As portrayed by the Memphites, Ptah was more a spirit than an anthropomorphic being. All the gods—those of Heliopolis and Hermopolis—were really aspects of Ptah. Ptah here is perhaps closer to the Abrahamic idea of God or even more so to the Hindu concept of the all-pervading essence of being, Brahman, than to the other Egyptian concepts of the creator. Ptah was the original spirit on the primeval mound, the "self-begotten." As Ewa Wasilewska puts it, "in him all divine forces were encoded" (65). He was Ptah-Nun (Niu) and Ptah Naunet, the primal watery abyss, the parents of Atum. In Atum's form the heart and tongue of Ptah "came into being." The gods of the Ennead were the teeth and lips of Ptah. Horus, in this case the sun god, the god of command, represented his heart, and the moon god Thoth, the god of intelligence and wisdom, was his tongue. The gods were conceived in Ptah's heart and given their *ka*s or inner essences by him. The gods were named, and thus given form, by Ptah's tongue. Ptah, like the Old Testament God in Genesis, created by thought and word. He *was* the Word, the Logos.

Clark points out that as the Egyptians understood things, the "heart and the voice-organ, determine the actions of men and animals . . . so God is the heart and tongue of his Creation" (Clark, 62). By extension the individual essences (*kas*) of human beings come from the Word, which is Ptah, and the world itself is of Ptah.

The Theban Creation

Texts dating to the New Kingdom period of Ramses II (1279–1213 B.C.E.) reveal the Theban high god Amun, later Amun-Re, as the creator. Amun, we are told, was the "invisible one" of unknown origins, with no parents to establish his name or *ka*. As such, he had no external identity and was invisible even to the other gods, who were aspects of him. From Amun's mysterious being came the gods of Hermopolis and then those of Heliopolis—"the Ennead is combined in your body" (Allen, 24). A later version of the story says that Amun in his form as Ptah created the primal egg in the primal waters of Nun and that he fertilized the egg, and the other gods emerged from it (Wasilewska, 66). Once again, as in other Egyptian creations, especially the Memphite creation, the tendency at Thebes is toward an all-informing single God who, like the Hindu Brahman, takes many forms, a tendency furthered by Akhenaton's cult of the Aton as the only creator and, according to some, the only god.

The Creation of Humans

As Ewa Wasilewska so clearly points out (136–42), the Egyptian theologians in general seem to have had little interest in the creation of humans. They were clearly more concerned with larger questions relating to cosmic arrangements, kingship, and the afterlife. There are a few texts, however, that present various ideas of our origins.

In Spell 80 of the Coffin Texts, Shu, who is air, is also regarded as life itself. He literally breathes life into the nostrils of humans and other animals, completing a process that also includes the ancient naming ritual:

> I will lead them and enliven them,
> Through my mouth, which is Life in their nostrils.
> I will lead my breath into their throats, after I have tied on their
>   head by the Annunciation that is in my mouth.
> (Allen, 13)

Wasilewska outlines the two primary traditions surrounding the creation of humans: creation by the god's tears and creation by clay. In both the Atum and the later Amun theologies we find the tear motif. According to the Coffin Texts Atum created the gods out of his sweat and humans out of his tears; in the later version it was from Amun-Re's eyes that "mankind came forth." In the case of Atum, the creation of humans seems to have been accidental. When Atum's eye disappeared one day, Shu and Tefnut brought it back, and when the eye was replaced in Atum he wept, and "that is the evolution of people" (Allen, 15). Wasilewska points out that the Egyptian words for "people" and "tears" were similar. It would seem likely that the association of tears with people might suggest a certain sadness implicit in mortality.

Wasilewska makes a strong case for the lost eye being the great goddess Hathor, who would then have played an important role with Atum in the creation of humans (138). Hathor figured prominently in the creation-from-clay motif contained in the myth of the southern god Khnum. As the ram-headed god—the word for "ram" being equivalent to the word for "soul"—Khnum was the soul of the high god Amun-Re. Khnum was the creator in one of the myths that evolved around the usurper queen Hatshepsut. He was said to have created the queen and her *ka* out of clay on his potter's wheel, and then to have placed her in her mother's womb to be born as Amun-Re's daughter. It was believed by some that humans in general were conceived in this manner and that after Khnum completed the forms, Hathor would provide life by touching them with her ankh, the Egyptian crosslike symbol of life itself.

As to the purpose of humans in the world, there is little information. In the instructions left in c. 2040 B.C.E., during the period between the Old and Middle Kingdoms, by the king of Herakleopolis to his son Merikare, we learn that humans are "god's cattle" but also that they are "his images who came from his body" (Hallo, 65).

Wasilewska reminds us of a similar sense of humans being made "in the image of God" that would emerge in the Hebrew Genesis (141).

Osiris and Isis

The dominant myth in Egypt for over three thousand years was that of the god Osiris and his sister-wife Isis. Of all the Egyptian deities

these two were the ones most closely associated with the world of human beings. As a victim and dying god, Osiris shared the human experience of mortality. This fact made him a mythological brother, as it
were, of other Middle Eastern dying gods, including Dumuzi, Adonis, Attis, Dionysos, Telipinu, and Jesus. It was through Osiris and
these others that humans in various cultures hoped to join the universal process of nature that involved afterlife or rebirth after apparent
death. So it was that Osiris was associated with the Nile and its annual revival of the land through the death that was the flood. And it
was Osiris whose revival was reflected in the grain rising from the
earth. This was the god of all kinds of fertility.

Significantly, Osiris was the first pharaoh—a king in this world in a
mythological golden age. As such, he was more of a material being,
more tangible than the other gods. He was an example of god become
man. As the ruler at the world's beginning, Osiris gave human society—
that is to say, Egypt—law and civilization. The golden age came to an
end when Osiris's brother Seth introduced death by killing his
brother and depriving the world for a time of his potency and fertility.
There are many versions of the manner in which this primordial murder was accomplished. Some say that Seth became a flea whose bite
poisoned Osiris. Others say Seth threw his brother into the sea. A
more common story, told much later by the Greek writer Plutarch
(c. 46–120 C.E.), tells how Seth tricked Osiris into lying in a special
coffin, after which he and his cohorts closed the lid and flung the
coffin into the water. The coffin floated to the shore of Byblos in
Phoenicia, where a tree formed around it, tying the god-hero once
again to other Middle Eastern figures associated with trees. Adonis,
Attis, Dionysos, and Jesus were all in one way or another imprisoned
in or on trees.

The tree of Osiris, a symbol of renewed potency to come, was particularly sweet-smelling and grew very large—perhaps like the *linga*
of Siva or the fruit tree that emerged from Dionysos's loins. It
pleased the king of the region, who had it cut down for use as a column in his new palace. The column with a hermlike erection pro-
truding from it was one of many symbols of Osiris. The column
attracted the attention of Isis, who had traveled the world in search
of her beloved husband.

It is at this point that Isis emerges as a principal figure, taking her place among the great goddesses of Egypt. Isis managed to obtain the column containing the coffin from the king, and she removed her husband's body and returned with it to Egypt. Although Isis attempted to hide her husband's body in Egypt, Seth found it and cut it into many pieces before flinging it into the Nile. Isis managed to retrieve the pieces of the body—all, according to Plutarch, but the penis, the symbol of fertility itself, which was eaten by a fish, another symbol of fertility.

After retrieving the pieces of her husband's body, Isis, helped by her sister (Seth's wife) Nephthys (and Anubis, according to some), repaired the body as the first Egyptian mummy and through various spells managed to revive it sufficiently for Isis to fly over it as a bird and to conceive Horus, presumably from the seed of the erect phallus that sprang plantlike from the dead king. Isis gave birth to Horus in the delta and hid him away until such time as he would be ready to avenge her husband's murder. Meanwhile, Osiris descended to the underworld, where he would remain in a passive state until his son could avenge him. In a sense Osiris was resurrected in his form as the grain god. It was said that Isis "planted" symbols of his missing phallus in many burial shrines all over Egypt, thus spreading his cult and ensuring the fertility of the land (see Clark, 97ff.).

Horus and Seth

The struggle between Horus and Seth is metaphorically related not only to the establishment of the early dynasties in Egypt and the struggle between north and south mentioned earlier, but, in connection with Osiris, to the whole question of the sacred kingship in Egypt. The old king died as Osiris, and the new king reigned as Horus, who had defeated the disorder of Seth.

According to the myth, when Horus grew into manhood he and his followers attacked Seth, who had usurped Osiris's throne. The struggle was acutely disturbing to universal order. Horus pulled out the testicles of his uncle, and Seth took out his nephew's eye. It was up to Thoth, the god of proper order, to convince the combatants to agree to arbitration. The gods decided in Horus's favor, and Horus was made the new king. Horus then traveled to the underworld to

take his retrieved eye to Osiris as a symbol of the reestablishment of
proper order. Through this visit the soul of Osiris and, thus, fertility
were revived. As Clark writes, "Osiris was nothing without Horus,
just as the latter was no true king unless he was able to guarantee the
fertility of the land. . . . It is Horus who fulfills the destiny for the present, undertaking the role played in other religions by the resurrected
god" (108). As for Seth, he became Osiris's boat or the breeze that
propels the dead king's boat on ritual voyages on the Nile.

The Egyptian Flood

The Egyptian flood story resembles the Mesopotamian and the Genesis flood stories in that it tells the story of the ungrateful evil of humankind, the punishment for that evil, and the saving of a few in order
that a new beginning might be made. A late-third-millennium B.C.E.
myth of the Herakleopolitan dynasties tells how humankind plotted
against the high god Re, and Re called into council his "eye" (the goddess Hathor) and the other important gods "who were with me in the
Primeval Waters," including the original god of the watery chaos, Nun
himself (Clark, 181ff.). Re asked advice of Nun. What was he to do
about these misguided humans, the children of his "eye"? Nun advised
that he turn his "eye" against humankind, and the other gods agreed.
And so the "eye," as the now Kali-like destructive Hathor (perhaps the
hot, unbridled sun), descended upon humans and killed them in the
desert. Hathor returned claiming that to destroy mankind was "pleas-
ant to my heart." The "eye" as the lion goddess Sekhmet was sent to
continue the destruction, but Re decided to prevent total destruction.
He created beer from barley and red ochre and flooded the fields of
Egypt with it. Sekhmet, on her way to the slaughter, was attracted by
the beer and drank so much of it that she became intoxicated and for-
got about killing humans. So it was that a few were saved.

Hero Myths of the Egyptians

Hero myths such as those found in Greece or Rome or even Mesopotamia are not common in ancient Egypt. Heroism as such seems to
be inextricably tied to the themes of sacred kingship in relation to the

sun's journey across the sky and the idea of the king's and later any individual's passage after death to the underworld. At the center of
what might be called the one Egyptian hero myth is Horus.

Horus as Hero

In a sense the pharaoh, who lived as Horus, was always a god-hero
who at death made the heroic journey to the sky to join Re on his solar bark and to guard him against serpents and other perils there during the daily journey from horizon to horizon. In this context we need
to remember that one of Horus's titles was "son of Re," so that the
pharaoh, like Horus himself, was the son of the god to whom he returned after a sojourn on earth. The myth of Horus justifies the sacred kingship. Hero myths in general reflect human concerns and are
expressive of that post mythological period when the high god—in
this case Re—retreats to a kind of seclusion in the heavens and no
longer communicates directly with humans. Not surprisingly, then,
many of the myths of Horus himself—the god who, with Isis and
Osiris, had most to do with human life—have more in common with
traditional hero myths than with deity myths. Like those of another
man-god, Jesus, they contain all of the essential elements of Joseph
Campbell's monomyth. We have already seen that Horus was miraculously conceived, that his quest was to restore the "kingdom" of his father in a struggle with monstrous evil represented by his nemesis
Seth. And we have seen that Horus is, in a sense, Osiris reborn.
Osiris's resurrection as Horus represents the possibility of any individual's succeeding on the traditional heroic journey into the underworld. The *Book of Two Ways* tells us that a dead person who has
learned the proper spells of the first stage of afterlife will join the
moon god Thoth as a star.

Thoth also plays the traditional role of the hero's guide in the
afterlife. If he knows the second stage of spells, the deceased will go
to the underworld palace of Osiris. And if he learns the third stage of
spells, he will accompany Re on his bark across the sky; in short, he
will go to the "Father in Heaven" (Lesko, "Egyptian Religion," 41).
Clark supports this concept of the heroic pilgrimage of the soul after
death when he points out that the Coffin Texts assumed "the soul's

visit to Osiris at the end of the journey or a series of initiations during
which the Horus soul-figure has acquired the superlative qualities of a
hero—might, glory, strength, power and divinity." Clark goes on to
compare Osiris to the Fisher King of Arthurian lore, whose "wound"
must be cured by the words—in this case the proper spells—of the
Grail hero (Clark, 161–62, and see Joseph Campbell, *Hero*, 368ff.).

A hauntingly familiar aspect of the Horus story exists in the so-
called Delta Cycle. After conceiving a child by her partially revived
husband, Isis retreated from the evil usurper king, Seth, into hiding in
the swamps of the delta. In that hidden and unglamorous place she
gave birth to Horus. Many things happened to the divine child during his days in the delta. While his mother was off begging for food,
he was attacked and bitten by Seth disguised as serpents, for instance.
But the Pyramid Texts tell us that the holy infant "with his finger in
his mouth" stamped on the serpent "with his foot" (Clark 187). Later,
from the wilderness of the swamps, a place called Chemmis, the
young man Horus went to the underworld to visit his father and then
on to the great struggle with Seth. Clark suggests that Horus in these
stories is the "essential hero who is destined to bring back order to the
whole universe" (187).

8

The Mythology of Anatolia

The mythology of pre-Greek and pre-Islamic Anatolia (Asia Minor, Asian Turkey) is an amalgamation of the pantheons and sacred stories of several peoples, including the Hattians, the Hittites, and the Hurrians. The Hattians, or proto-Hattians (since the Hittites took on the Hattic name), were an indigenous people who were living on the central Anatolian plateau when the Hittites and several smaller Indo-European tribes, the Luwians and Palaians, arrived there at the end of the third millennium B.C.E. The Hurrians, while politically and geographically more Mesopotamian than Anatolian, made significant inroads into Anatolia, and their religion forms a major part of the Hittite-Anatolian mythology. Other Mesopotamian mythic material and Canaanite stories as well also found their way into Anatolian mythology by way of the Hurrians.

The religiously tolerant Hittites attempted to make sense of the many deities that they accepted into their official pantheon. Near the Hittite capital of Hattusa, at a place called Yazılıkaya, is a second-millennium B.C.E. open stone gallery in which a procession of gods and goddesses is carved. These are the "thousand gods of Hatti," a collection of old Hattian, Hittite, and Hurrian divinities, many identified in a hieroglyphic script developed by the Luwians.

The Pantheons

The deities assimilated by the Hittites from the indigenous Hattians are somewhat unclear to modern scholars because of the still scant knowledge of the Hattic language. The Hattian pantheon seems to have been a collection of personifications of aspects of nature (such as Estan, meaning "sun" or "day," and Kasku, meaning "moon") and expressions of life forces represented by mother goddesses (Kattahha, Hannahanna the "grandmother," Kubaba, Wurusemu), war god–kings (Wurrunkatte, Zababa, Kattishabi), and a weather or storm god (Taru). Deities derived from the Hurrians, on the other hand, were more endowed with human characteristics, not always noble ones, and were clearly influenced by the old Mesopotamian deities.

High Gods and Mother Goddesses

The old Hattian mother goddess, with roots at least as deep as the concept of the great goddess depicted in nearby Neolithic Çatal Hüyük, was the source of life and a natural mate for the Anatolian storm god, himself a close mythical relative of Zeus, Indra, Thor, and other familiar Indo-European sky gods, perhaps especially those of eastern Europe. An important function of the storm god was to constantly fight to retain his power at the top of the pantheon. In this aspect also, he resembles other Indo-European high gods and storm gods.

In their specifically Hittite form the great goddess and the high god became the sun goddess of Arina—originally Estan, later Hebat among the Hurrians—and the weather god of Hatti, sometimes called Taru in Old Hatti, Tarhunna among the Hittites, and Tesub (Tessub) by the Hurrians. The high god, whatever his name, was symbolized, like so many Middle Eastern high gods, by the bull. His consort was always a mother goddess such as Wurusemu, the wife of the Hattic Taru. At Hattusa the weather god was the city deity. The sun goddess at first seems to have shared that honor as his consort. The patriarchal Hittites and Hurrians thought of the sun as male, however, and under them there was a definite moving away from the old Hattic understanding. The Hittites referred to "our god Siu" (same root as *Zeus*, meaning "light of heaven"), and the Hurrians worshiped the sun as the male Simigi.

Still, the sun goddess of Arina, syncretized by the mid-second millennium with the Hurrian Hebat, the "queen of heaven," clearly leads the procession of goddesses at Yazılıkaya and might possibly have been differentiated from the male sun god by being designated a sun-goddess of the underworld, an aspect supported by the Hurrian-Hittite assimilation of the Babylonian Allatu (Inanna's underworld sister Ereshkigal) as the underworld sun goddess Allani. In any case, certainly in the Old Kingdom the sun goddess was the Anatolian mother of fertility. If her ancestor was the goddess of Çatal Hüyük, her later Anatolian relatives were the great Phrygian goddess Kybele, the mother of the sacrificed Attis, and the famous many-breasted Artemis of Ephesus (Wasilewska, 103–4; Leick, 155).

Lesser Goddesses

The mother goddess and the storm god had two daughters: Mezulla, who served as an intermediary between the human and divine worlds, and Inara, who was enlisted by her father to help in his struggle against the chaotic forces who would overthrow him (Leick, 93–94, 118).

Another Hurrian-Hittite goddess of importance was Sausga, a mythological relative of Inanna-Ishtar in Mesopotamia. Sausga was both a warrior and a love goddess. Like Devi in India, she had aspects of fertility (e.g., Parvati) as well as of destruction (Kali).

A goddess of magical powers was Kamrusepa, a deity of Luwian origin, who among the Hattians was Kattahziwuri, and who was associated with curing spells and with the myth of the disappearing god.

The Primeval Gods

These were the original deities in the story of the evolution of the gods. The Hurrians probably equated them with the Mesopotamian Anunnaki. They included some familiar Sumero-Babylonian gods—Anu and Enlil, for instance—and were cast aside by the storm god and his associates. As in Greece, where Zeus emerged from an ancient struggle involving first Uranos and then Kronos, the Hittite-Hurrian weather god was the end product of a process by which the original father god, Alalu, was overthrown by his servant or son Anu, and Anu was defeated by *his* son Kumarbi.

The Disappearing God

The Anatolian equivalent of the dying-god motif that we find in Egypt, Greece, and Canaan is the myth of the disappearing god, a pattern that also has relatives in such descent disappearances as those of Persephone in Greece and Inanna and Dumuzi in Sumer. The best-known Hittite god who disappeared is Telipinu, an ancient Hattic agricultural deity whose father was the dominant storm god. Other disappearing gods included the storm god himself, the sun god, and the earth goddess Hannahanna. The disappearing-god myths were associated with a Hittite ritual called the *mugawar*, intended to appease an angry god in order to restore order to the land and its people.

Anatolian Myths

Anatolian "Creation" and Hero Myths

We have scant knowledge of Anatolian creation myths. Fragments exist concerning the creation of humankind by Hittite Gulses, goddesses of fate who also watched over births (Wasilewska, 151). Creation themes rather than creation stories per se are found in the Hattian-Hittite stories of the storm god and the monstrous serpent Illuyanka and in the Hurrian-Hittite tales of the early god Kumarbi. Both of these myth cycles are concerned with the struggle between order and chaos that is at the center of most creation myths.

The Illuyanka Cycle

Two Illuyanka myths exist. In the first, the storm god is defeated in a battle at Kiskilussa (an actual place in Anatolia) by the serpent Illuyanka. The storm god's reaction to this defeat is to call for a feast, almost certainly representing the Hattian-Hittite *Purulli* festival in honor of the prosperity and fertility of the land and its people. The god's daughter Inara, as instructed by her father, provides the feast (including an abundance of wine and beer), symbolizing the fertility of the land. But the serpent remains a constant threat, and it seems to be up to the powerful goddess to overcome it. To accomplish her mission she apparently is in need of a human monster-tricking hero to assist her. She calls on one Hupasiya, who agrees to help in return for sexual favors. The goddess agrees, and after sleeping with Hupasiya, she hides her lover, approaches the serpent hole, and entices the monster to come out to join the feast she has prepared. The serpent and his family fall for the trick, emerge from their lair, and proceed to become so drunk that Hupasiya is able to burst out of his hiding place to tie them up. Then the storm god himself comes and kills them and creation is preserved.

The story continues in a fairy-tale-like mode. Inara is apparently fond of her human lover. One day, as she is leaving the house she has built for him, she warns him not to look out of the window. If he does, she says, he will see his neglected wife and children. Naturally, after some time he does look out of the window, and just as predictably he sees his wife and children, whom he longs to rejoin. He begs Inara—as Odysseus had begged Calypso, for example—to be allowed to go back home. The existing text is unclear as to whether he dies or is allowed to leave (Wasilewska, 105; Hoffner, *Hittite Myths*, 12).

The second Illuyanka tale says that the serpent defeated the storm god and stole his heart and eyes, thus threatening creation itself (and reminding us of the Horus myth in Egypt). The storm god then married a woman of the lower classes who provided him with a son. The son grew up and married a daughter of the serpent, and the storm god instructed him to request the missing heart and eyes as a dowry. The son did as he was instructed, and so the storm god regained his heart and eyes. Whole again, the storm god from his position in the sky attacked the serpent in the sea and succeeded in killing him. The storm god's son announced his loyalty to his father-in-law, so the storm god killed him, too (Hoffner, *Hittite Myths*, 13).

Ewa Wasilewska rightly points out that although these stories are apparently of proto-Hattic origin, they reflect the common Indo-European creation struggle between order and chaotic evil that would have made them popular with the Indo-European Hittites (Wasilewska, 105).

The Kumarbi Cycle

The later Hittites, under Hurrian influence, told the myths of Kumarbi that parallel the war-in-heaven myths of other Indo-European cultures, including the Greek and Vedic, a fact perhaps attributable to the midmillennium rule of the Mitanni kingdom by an Indo-European Aryan aristocracy. In any case, the war-in-heaven motif is a common feature in creation myths of all parts of the world; it serves as an explanation of the way the present world order came about. It also serves, as in the case of the Hurrian-Hittite version, to express the superiority of one culture's gods over those of a rival culture.

The Hurrians said that in the distant past Alalu was king of the gods and was served by the powerful Anu (the ancient Mesopotamian deity—sometimes An), according to some his son. But after nine years Anu overcame his father, who fled to the darkness of earth. Anu himself reigned for only nine years, during which time he was served by his son Kumarbi. In the last year of his reign Anu was overcome by the power of Kumarbi's eyes and hands, and he tried to flee into the sky in defeat. But Kumarbi reached up, pulled him back by his feet, and bit off his testicles. Kumarbi laughed at his father, who turned to him and suggested that his laughter might be foolish given the consequences of his act. By eating his father's testicles Kumarbi had been impregnated with the storm god Tesub, the Aranzah River, the noble Tasmisu, and two other frightening gods. Tesub was born and grew to manhood, and after Kumarbi tried and failed to eat him, he became king of the gods. Later Tesub would be defeated by Lamma, who was supported by the old primeval gods led by Ea. Later he, too, would be deposed. This whole struggle for kingship is central to the Hurrian worldview. It is a struggle between earth and sky—Alalu having been of the earth and Anu of the sky.

The Disappearance of Telipinu

The best known and most complete of the otherwise relatively fragmentary Old Anatolian myths is that of Telipinu (Telepinu), a Hittite myth with Old Hattian origins.

Telipinu was the son of the great storm or weather god. His myth, like other disappearing-god myths, was apparently intended to accompany rituals intended to soothe the anger of the gods—particularly that of the storm god—during times of trouble (Leick, 156–57; Hoffner, "Hittite Religion," 410). Although an agricultural deity responsible for the care and irrigation of the fields, Telipinu had the basic characteristics of his father and was referred to as a disappearing storm god capable of great anger and destruction (Hoffner, *Hittite Myths*, 14; Kramer, *Mythologies*, 144ff.; Leick, 156–57).

For some reason Telipinu became violently angered, so he put on his shoes and disappeared. Immediately the world lost its ability to function—the gods at their altars and the domestic animals in their pens were "stifled." Animals rejected their young, and all fertility ceased; the land dried up, and humans and gods alike suffered greatly. The storm god realized that his son's absence was the cause of the problem. The sun god sent out an eagle to search for Telipinu, but he could not find him anywhere—not in the sea, not on the mountains, not in the valleys. The storm god sought the advice of the ancient Hannahanna, the grandmother of goddesses. She suggested that the storm god go out himself in search of his vanished son. But in his attempt to leave his city, the storm god broke his hammer trying unsuccessfully to open the gate, so Hannahanna sent a bee to search for the god. The storm god was skeptical of the capabilities of so small a creature, but the bee departed on its mission. In time the bee found Telipinu asleep in a grove in a place called Lihzina (a famous storm god cult center). Awakened by the bee's sting, the god became furious, demonstrating all of his storm god power, causing horrible destruction everywhere. He struck the Dark Earth with ferocity. In desperation, the gods turned to the magician goddess Kamrusepa for help. She used magic spells, rituals, and formulas to soothe Telipinu and to revive his benevolent spirit.

The role of Kamrusepa, who performs a mythical representation of the *mugawar* ritual, is similar to that of the shaman or perhaps the therapist. She "takes his anger and his sullenness" from the disappearing god ("his soul and essence were stifled [like burning] brushwood") and makes that soul whole again. Under the spell of the ritual, "Telipinu let anger go"; it was "seized" by the Dark Earth.

Telipinu returned to his home, cleansed the destroyed land, and restored fertility and harmony. Mothers returned to the care of their children. Telipinu brought "Longevity and Progeny" back to the world. In all of this was "the Gentle Message of the Lamb . . . Plenty, Abundance, and Satiety" (Hoffner, *Hittite Myths*, 16–18).

9

The Mythology of the
Western Semites

The Western Semites were the Semitic-speaking peoples of the area that includes what was once known as the land of Canaan. In the pre-Islamic ancient world, Western Semites included Arameans, the various people labeled Canaanites (including the Phoenicians and the people of Ugarit), the Hebrew-Israelites, and other tribes that migrated to the region. The Western Semites produced both Judaism and Christianity.

Aramean Mythology

By the eleventh century B.C.E. Arameans, who had been in the area at least since the third millennium B.C.E., controlled northern Syria. With their capital at Damascus, they were a major force in the Middle East until their defeat by the Assyrians in the eighth and seventh centuries B.C.E. Even after their defeat, however, the Arameans retained significant cultural influence through their language and mythology. Because of the efficiency of the Aramaic alphabet as opposed to cuneiform, Aramaic became the diplomatic and commercial lingua franca of the Neo-Assyrian empire. Population exchanges after the Assyrians defeated Israel in 722 B.C.E. made Aramaic the common language of the Samaria and Galilee areas of that country. Later it served as the vernacular language of the exiles in Babylon and of the

85

returnees to Israel in the sixth century. The position of the language was solidified by the arrival in the sixth century of the Persians, who used Aramaic as their administrative language. Although Hebrew remained the literary language of the Jews, their common language for some time was Aramaic. This was so much the case that in the fifth century B.C.E. Aramaic translations of the Bible (*targumin*) were deemed necessary. Jesus spoke Aramaic; later, Syriac, an eastern Aramaic dialect, became an important liturgical and literary language of Middle Eastern Christians.

Although little is known of it, Aramean mythology, dominated by the benevolent weather-storm-fertility god Hadad, seems at first to have been significantly different from that of either the Mesopotamians or the Canaanites, Israelites, and other tribes in the area. Gradually, however, under Assyrian dominance, much of Mesopotamian religion was assimilated into Aramean beliefs, and still later, during the fourth century B.C.E., under the Seleucids, there is strong Phoenician and Greek influence.

Canaanite Mythology

So-called Canaanite mythology was that of the Western Semites in the land in and around modern Palestine, Israel, Lebanon, coastal Syria, and western Jordan at the time of the Israelite migration there from Egypt. According to the Genesis (9:18–22) myth, Canaan (Kan'an) was the son of Noah's son Ham, who was cursed for having seen his father's genitals. It was the descendants of Canaan who were said to have originally settled in the land to which they gave their name. We associate Canaanite culture, because of modern archeological finds, particularly with the people of the Amorite city of Mari on the border between modern Syria and Iraq, with the people who inhabited the Ugarit site (Ras Shamra) in the coastal region of what is now Syria, and with the coastal peoples the Greeks called the Phoenicians, who lived in what is now Lebanon. In addition, numerous Canaanite tribes are listed in Genesis (10:15–20) among the Israelite conquests in the land of Canaan. Much of Canaanite mythology was adopted by the non-Semitic Philistines, who became the primary rival of the Israelites for conquest of Canaan. When we speak of Canaanite mythology it is important to realize that it has come down to us in a limited form gleaned from archeological sites, biblical references, and literary fragments. That noted, it is fair to say that a somewhat consistent mythology does emerge.

Hebrew-Israelite and Jewish Mythology

The Israelites brought with them a mythology in the process of development that—although influenced at various periods by the mythologies of Egypt, by the indigenous religions of Canaan, and later by the traditions of the Babylonians—would follow a highly individual course. Probably closer in spirit to the mythology of the Hebrews were those of other small neighboring clan-based tribes such as the Moabites, the Ammonites, and the Edomites, for instance, who spoke Canaanite languages related to Hebrew and who all had dominant patriarchal clan gods. A still more specific influence on the religion and mythology that would become Judaism was in all likelihood that of the Midianites in the northwestern Arabian Peninsula (modern Hijaz), people who were said to have provided the biblical hero Moses not only with a wife but with important elements of the Yahweh cult. The Midianite connection is suggested mythologically by the fact that the story of Yahweh speaking to Moses from the burning bush takes place in Midian (Exodus 2). Moshe Weinfeld sees a "proto-Israelite belief in Yahweh" among many of the nomadic tribes of Palestine and the Sinai (Weinfeld, 483–84). It might well be that the god of the Hebrews was the god of the Habiru, the many foreign nomads—including the Israelites—who for a time inhabited the Sinai and Negev regions.

The mythology of the Torah or "law," technically the first five books—the Pentateuch—of the Hebrew Bible, is traditionally attributed to Moses. Given the various versions of particular events and obvious changes in emphasis, style, and chronology in particular books, however, the actual composition of the Torah is now generally traced to several sources. The earliest is referred to as the Yahwist author, or simply J (from the German *Jahweh*), because of his use of the name Yahweh for the creator god in Genesis. J apparently wrote in southern Israel (Judah) during the early monarchy, that is, around 950 B.C.E. A rival document by an Elohist writer (E, because of the use of the term *Elohim* for the high god) was written in northern Israel in about 850 B.C.E., although it clearly makes use of much older oral material. The material of J and E were combined in about 750 B.C.E. Finally, exilic and post-exilic (587–400 B.C.E.) priestly writers, usually designated as P, assimilated and somewhat altered the J and E sources and added a great deal of material on genealogies, liturgies, temple ceremonies, and rules.

To the original Torah were added eventually the other books of the Jewish Bible, probably compiled by several writers, including an eighth-century-B.C.E. figure labeled by scholars as the Deuteronomic Historian or DH. The Pentateuch and the added books—the *Nevi'im* (Prophets), the *Ketuvim* (Writings), and the Apocrypha—form what some refer to now as a whole as the Torah and what Christians call the Old Testament to differentiate the Jewish scriptures from the purely Christian ones (New Testament) in the Christian Bible. The Christian form of the Bible, then, is a combination of Jewish and Christian scriptures.

Much of the mythology of the Hebrews, who in Canaan became known as Israelites and who established the foundations of Judaism, was clearly intended to justify the Hebrew conquest and settlement of Canaan eventually described in the first part of the *Nevi'im*, the "Former Prophets," containing six biblical books: Joshua, Judges, 1 and 2 Samuel, and 1 and 2 Kings. The justification of conquest is based on the belief in a single god who gradually emerged from the clan and tribal "god of Abraham." The mythology suggests that this god, later identified as Yahweh, favored the Hebrew-Israelites, and therefore the Jews, above all peoples of the earth. He favored them so much that even though Canaan was heavily populated by other peoples—most of them fellow Semites—it was only right that they should take it for themselves. This was so because the Lord had promised this land to his chosen people in a covenant made with the patriarch Abram (Abraham) and reaffirmed with Isaac, Jacob (Israel), and Moses. The special relationship of a sole and living deity directly with a whole people marked a significant change in the religion and mythology of the Middle East. Deities such as those of the Sumerians, Assyrians, Hittites, Canaanites, and Philistines were clearly metaphorical and therefore easily assimilated by various peoples at various times (including many of the pre-exilic Hebrew-Israelites, who required the teachings and admonitions of the patriarchs, judges, prophets, and priests to turn them away from "pagan" worship). But for Judaism as it developed, the divine was represented only by a jealous and not always compassionate god who had no divine rivals or companions. To the extent that they are fundamentalists, Jews, and later Christians and Muslims, tend to take the monotheistic god as a literal rather than metaphorical fact. For Jews especially, whose religion and nationhood are so intricately tied to a mythology that stresses lineage and the exclusivity of the race or tribe, the perceived reality of a covenant with the deity in the mythological past continues to affect the concept of nationhood and land rights in the Middle East today. The concept is clearly symbolized mythologically by the establishing by the patriarchs of altars to Yahweh specifically on sites sacred to the Canaanites in Hebron, Bethel, and elsewhere.

Christian Mythology

As for the Christians, their mythology, in the New Testament and various noncanonical or apocryphal gospels and writings and traditions, centers on the person of Jesus of Nazareth, a Jewish reformer whose god and "father" was the god of the Jews. As it evolved, Christian mythology was able indirectly to incorporate various aspects of Middle Eastern and Greek mythology, especially in relation to dying-god and hero motifs and that of the mother goddess. Most of all, however, Christianity is a religion that looks back to its Jewish roots but in so doing expands the possibility of redemption by extending the "kingdom" and the "promised land" beyond the Hebrew race or Jewish religion to the world at large. To the extent that the religion has insisted over the centuries that its way is the only way and/or that its myths are literally true, it has developed a militancy and a tendency toward fundamentalism that have often placed it at odds with the actual teachings of its de facto founder by instigating or supporting violence, abuse, and repression.

The Pantheons

Central to the Canaanite pantheon in its many local versions is a
movement toward an understanding of deity that includes a high god
associated with weather and storms who is somewhat distant from
everyday life, a fertility god who is more present, and a feminine form
of that deity. The Arameans, too, had their storm god with a strong
fertility aspect, and they assimilated several goddesses from Mesopotamia and Phoenicia. The Hebrews developed a god who reigned
alone as at once a weather-storm deity, a god of judgment, and a war
god, but who contained within himself aspects of the old deities who
concerned themselves with fertility and life on earth. For the Christians that god became a somewhat distant figure whose nevertheless
more loving purpose was to be accomplished by Jesus, a figure eventually seen as both human hero and an aspect of God. Christians, perhaps inadvertently, would over the centuries restore something of the
feminine to the godhead through the esoteric understanding of
Sophia, or divine wisdom—even for some the Holy Spirit aspect of
God—and especially through the person of the Virgin Mary.

The High God

A Semitic word for "god" is *el* or *il* (thus *Elohim* and *al-ilah* or *Allah*).
In second-millennium B.C.E. god lists found at Ugarit there are several Els or versions of El. There is the El of the holy mountain Sapan
(Tsafon); the Ilib (Elib), or "father god," who contains the spirits of
the dead; and the El who, like so many Near Eastern high gods, is associated with the bull and is perhaps the creator (Cooper, 37). The
Greeks thought of El as Kronos, the father of Zeus.

Dagan (Dagon) is another vehicle for the high-god concept, perhaps an early personification of El. He has fertility aspects, as his
name seems to mean "grain." Dagan existed at Ebla as early as the
third millennium B.C.E. and was assimilated as the high god of the
Philistines in the late second millennium.

It can be argued that the most important expression of the high god
in Canaan, however, was Baal in his many forms. But usually Baal took
second position to a father, sometimes El, sometimes Dagan. Baal was

at once a weather-storm god of great power and a dying god and fertilizer of the earth. For the Philistines he was Baalzebub, a healer, whom the Greeks associated with Asklepios. In a list of Phoenician deities contained in a 677 B.C.E. treaty between the king of Assyria and the king of Tyre he was the chief god, Baal-Shamen, the "lord of heaven," the El, the storm god, Baal-Safon of the Holy Mountain, Zeus of Phoenicia.

The Aramean high god, Hadad, was a counterpart of the Mesopotamian-Assyrian weather-storm-fertility god Adad. He was sometimes combined with or displaced by the Canaanite Baal—as Baal-Hadad or at least as the *baal,* or "lord." Later he was associated with the Greek Zeus and Roman Jupiter.

The god of the Hebrews dominates the myths of the Hebrew scriptures. This god, too holy to name, was expressed in the form of the tetragrammaton YHWH (usually transliterated as Yahweh or Yahveh), based on the verb for "to be"—thus he reveals himself to Moses as "I am." In later times the name of this god was not to be spoken, since to speak the name might release its power and bring about destruction. Rather, he is addressed as Adonai ("my Lord[s]") or Elohim ("the god[s]"). At first he may have been, like the Moabite Chemosh or the Canaanite Baal and numerous other Middle Eastern gods of the third and second millennia B.C.E., a tribal god among many gods. It seems apparent both from scriptural and historical sources that in common practice the Hebrews assimilated the gods and goddesses of Canaan. The lack of cohesion among the early Hebrews in Canaan made even monolatry—the exclusive worship of one god among many—an impossibility. The pull of polytheism was so strong that even the monarchy frequently succumbed to it. Monotheism (as opposed to monolatry) among the Israelites was not common until the time of the exile in Babylon and the reestablishment of Israel after the exile, that is, not until the sixth century B.C.E. And even then it can be argued that the firm establishment of monotheism in Judaism required the rabbinical or Talmudic input of the first century B.C.E. to the sixth century C.E.

Whether one among many or one alone, the god of the Hebrew Bible possessed many familiar Middle Eastern characteristics. He was a storm or weather god who could push aside the sea and lead with a

pillar of fire. He was a god of war who could mercilessly kill the enemies of the Israelites. He was a fertility god who could create the
world, replenish the earth after the flood, and make even the barren
Sarah bear a child. And he was a jealous god of judgment who expelled Adam and Eve from the Garden of Eden and punished his
chosen people for their sins. He was the god who denied humans a common language—through which they might become too powerful—by
destroying the Tower of Babel, the Babylonian ziggurat-temple (Genesis 11:1–9). He was the angry god who answered the much-maligned
Job "out of the tempest," asking him sarcastically, "Where were you
when I laid the earth's foundations?" (Job 38–41).

It seems almost certain that the god of the Jews evolved gradually
from the Canaanite El, who was in all likelihood the "god of Abraham."
Karen Armstrong reminds us that in Genesis 17, an eighth-century
B.C.E. text, God introduces himself to Abraham as El Shaddai (El of
the mountain), and that El's name is preserved in such words as *Elohim, Israel,* and *Ishmael* (Armstrong, *History of God,* 14). In Exodus
(6:2–3) the deity introduces himself to Moses as Yahweh and points
out that he had revealed himself to Abraham, Isaac, and Jacob as El
Shaddai and that they had not known that his name was Yahweh.

For Jewish mystics, the Kabbalists, God is seen as a mysterious entity called En (Ein) Sof, from the innermost recesses of which the
flame of divinity emerged at the beginning of time.

The early Christians in the Middle East were Jews for whom the
high god was the god of the Hebrew Scriptures. In his appearances in
the New Testament (the Christian books of the Bible), however, he
was less of a war god than in the Old Testament, less of a weather or
storm god. Rather, he was the loving and approving father of Jesus.
And it was Jesus as the Son of God who took up much of the role of
the old Jewish god who had concerned himself directly and sometimes in person with the activities of humans. In the Gospel of John
(1:1) he is seen as the Logos (the Word), or divine ordering principle,
which had existed from the beginning of time and which was equated
with God and was incarnated ("became flesh"), took human form, as
Jesus. Through Jesus and the spiritual presence of God as the Holy
Spirit, the Christian god evolved in post–New Testament times into a
complex philosophical construct known as the Trinity, in which God

has three aspects or "persons"—Father, Son, and Holy Spirit. Thus the Christian child learns that the Father, the Son, and the Holy Spirit are not each other but that the Father, the Son, and the Holy Spirit are mysteriously all God.

The Dying God

The motif of the dying god is a relatively universal one. It is closely related to the even more universal myth of the hero's descent into the underworld. Nearly always the god's apparent death results in some kind of rebirth or resurrection. The great dying god of Egypt was Osiris, who was revived by his wife, Isis, and who returned in the form of his son Horus and in the form of grain and the rejuvenated land after the annual Nilotic floods. Attis, the son of the great goddess Kybele of Phrygian Anatolia, was a dying god, as was Dionysos in Greece and, in a sense, Inanna and especially Dumuzi in Mesopotamia. In Ugaritic Canaan the dying god was Baal, the son of El or Dagan, who descended into the jaws of death (Mot) but who, with the help of the goddess Anat, returned and reestablished fertility for the land. In Phoenicia, Melqart, the city god of Tyre, was a dying and reviving god, as was Eshmun, the city deity of Sidon and Byblos. The best-known of the Canaanite dying gods was Adonis, the spring god of the Phoenicians, who also became popular in Greece and Rome as a human with whom Aphrodite-Venus fell in love. In his Greco-Roman form he was more a symbol of youthful sexuality than of spring. His name was related to *Adonai* ("my Lord").

The Middle Eastern version of the dying-god motif fully blossoms in the story of Jesus, who was said to have died and then returned to life after three days (one of them in hell), bringing the possibility of what might be called spiritual as opposed to physical fertility.

The Goddess

Among the Western Semites goddesses played a significant and sometimes dominant mythological role. Typically, the goddess in question makes concrete the abstract reality represented by her male consort. Thus the Phoenician Ashtart, known also as Ashtoret and in

Greek as Astarte, was the "name of Baal," and her equivalent in Carthage, Tinnit, was the "face of Baal." As William Fulco suggests, when Baal struggled against Mot that struggle represented the *fight* for fertility, while his consort (as Anat) was the actual *fighting* for fertility. And although El was for some Canaanites the father of creation, his consort, Athirat, was the "creatress of the gods" (Fulco, "Anat"). Something like this relationship between god and goddess exists in Vedic and Hindu India between the god and his *śakti*, the energizing material power of the god personified as his feminine consort.

The difficulty in isolating the Western Semitic goddesses from each other is indicated by the similarity of their names, their common role as consorts to the high gods, their role as fertility goddesses, and by the fact that the various cities and tribes assimilated and combined each other's mythological figures. Thus the often violent and overtly sexual Anat was the Canaanite consort of Baal and was later fused with Ashtart-Ashtoret-Astarte to become Atargatis, the goddess whom the Greeks associated with Aphrodite and who was known to the Romans as Dea Syria. In Hebrew she was Asherah, a blend of Anat, Ashtart, and the more motherly Athirat (the Ugaritic consort of El), and was also reminiscent of the old Mesopotamian Inanna-Ishtar. It might be argued that the many Western Semitic goddesses can be seen as aspects of the one great goddess.

As a fertility goddess, Asherah, like the fertility god Baal (or gods—*baalim*), was attractive to the Israelites when they moved from a nomadic lifestyle to an agricultural one. Asherah was represented by phallic objects called *asherim* and prayed to at particular cult places. If El was the high god of Abraham—Elohim, the prototype of Yahweh—Asherah was his wife, and there are archeological indications that she was perceived as such before she was in effect "divorced" in the context of emerging Judaism in the seventh century B.C.E. (see 2 Kings 23:15; Wasilewska, 113). Many of the Hebrew prophets saw in the popular goddess cult a real threat to the Yahweh religion. Jeremiah condemned the Israelite worship of the so-called queen of heaven, who was thought to ensure fecundity (Jeremiah 7:44).

There was no place for a sexual pagan goddess consort in the concept of a god who reigned alone as the special patron of the Israelites.

Even when certain kings of Israel advocated the worship of Baal or the *baalim* for agricultural purposes, the worship of the goddess seems to have been perceived as a threat to the community, certainly to its patriarchal arrangements (see 1 Kings 18:17–19).

An indication of an earlier view perhaps exists in Proverbs (8:22–31), where Wisdom, personified as a woman, is said to have been with Yahweh during the creation. The role of Wisdom in this context may be said to resemble that of the Canaanite goddesses who became the active agents of the reality of the gods. Furthermore, in Jewish mysticism there is the tradition of the *shekhinah*, the feminine form of the divine. The original Hebrew word referred to the Lord's presence in the temple at Jerusalem and elsewhere. For some, the *shekhinah* as God's feminine aspect is thought to be present especially during the twenty-four hours of the Sabbath.

As for the Christians, they in effect, if not theologically, gradually restored the "queen of heaven" to her ancient position as goddess. They did so in the person of Mary, the mother of Jesus. But as they mythologized this once simple Jewish maiden, the wife of a carpenter, and made her their chief intercessor with God in heaven, Christians deprived her of the sexuality once associated with the western Semitic goddess. She became the immaculately conceived Virgin Mary, who was herself impregnated immaculately by God as the Holy Spirit. Mary took on the mythological role of mother of God in his aspect as Jesus and was assumed into heaven to reign there as immaculate intercessor queen, but decidedly not as wife, with God the Father. Some Christians and Gnostics also incorporated the feminine into their sense of deity in the person of the divine wisdom of Proverbs as Sophia—thus the great church of Saint Sophia in Constantinople (modern Istanbul).

The Cosmic Myths

The Canaanite Creation

Little is known of the prebiblical Western Semitic creation myths, but creation is suggested in various Ugaritic fragments. These texts imply that El earned the title "creator" and "father of the gods" by defeating his parents, Heaven and Earth. Having taken over the creator role, El became the head of the Canaanite pantheon, the source of virility without which life was not possible. One Ugaritic tablet tells how in ancient times as El stood at the seashore his hand (penis) grew as long as the sea itself. With him were two women, his wives, whom he kissed and impregnated simultaneously. They gave birth to dawn and dusk (Coogan, *Encyclopedia* 3:51). On the other hand, El's wife, as noted above, also held the titles of creatrix and "mother of the gods," titles that presumably came with her role as El's consort and activating aspect (see Wasilewska, 110–18).

It is in the so-called Baal Cycle that we find more complex and complete stories suggesting creation, or at least the early establishment of divine order through the kind of war in heaven that also exists in Anatolian, Mesopotamian, Hebrew, Christian, and other Middle Eastern mythologies, as well as in the mythologies of Indo-Europeans. It is clear that by the late second millennium B.C.E., Baal, like Marduk in Mesopotamia, had taken over the position at the head of the pantheon, El having withdrawn from active participation in the affairs of creation. But this withdrawal was a gradual process involving a great struggle and a descent by Baal into death itself.

The Baal Cycle opens with the demand of Yamm, the sea and river god ("Prince Sea" or "Judge River")—perhaps a male equivalent of the Mesopotamian female Tiamat, who was destroyed by Marduk—that Baal accept his supremacy. Yamm is supported in this demand by the ancient father god El, who apparently is allied with Yamm in his attempt to prevent Baal from achieving supremacy among the gods. El commissions Yamm to fight Baal, as the Hurrian-Hittite Kumarbi had commissioned Ullikummi to fight Tesub. As Yahweh, "with his strong arm . . . cleft the sea monster . . . struck down Rahab with his skill" (Job 26:12), Baal successfully battles Yamm, using sacred thunderbolt weapons made by the craft god, and he dismembers his enemy as Marduk dismembered Tiamat. Baal "destroys Judge River," as Yahweh caused the Sea of Reeds to part for the Hebrews. The goddess Ashtart (Astarte) proclaims Baal's new status: "Hail, Baal the Conqueror! / hail Rider on the Clouds" (Coogan, *Stories*, 76).

Meanwhile, Baal's sister-wife Anat has been violently subduing enemies of Baal—so violently, in fact, that Baal calls her off and tricks her into returning to his side, presumably so that she will not destroy the whole world. This situation is reminiscent of the Egyptian god Re's having to recall the goddess Hathor-Sekhmet from her destructive rampage. Upon Anat's return, Baal announces that he requires a palace commensurate with his new status. Anat agrees to help in convincing their father, El, to allow the construction of such a palace, but to obtain permission Anat and Baal have to use bribery to gain the support of El's consort Athirat (Asherah). Ewa Wasilewska and others suggest that the building of Baal's palace, like the building of Marduk's temple and Yahweh's temple (2 Samuel 5–7; 1 Kings) is a metaphor for creation process and for the belief that "Baal re-establishes existing principles and preserves the order of existence" (Wasilewska, 116).

During the building of Baal's palace a dispute arises over the question of a window. The architect god Kothar wants to install one, but Baal, almost certainly because of the ancient superstition that death enters a home through a window, refuses to have one installed. It is only after more military victories and a great celebratory banquet in the palace that the god agrees to a window. Once it is constructed Baal proclaims his new position of dominance as the storm god and refuses to pay the tribute traditionally offered to death.

The final episode of the cycle is concerned with the struggle between Mot (death) and Baal (life). Invited by Mot to descend to the underworld, Baal cannot refuse. After mating eighty-eight times with a heifer—perhaps Anat, as in the Middle East, as we have seen, the head god is frequently depicted as a bull and the goddess as a cow—Baal enters the underworld and is, from the world's point of view, dead. Baal has taken his children and the elements of his storm god-ship with him. The world thus is deprived of weather and fertility. Anat, El, and the other gods mourn and wonder what will happen to the world without the divine energy that is Baal, the "lord of the earth." The faithful Anat, like Isis in Egypt, springs into action. She confronts Mot, who says he has devoured Baal, and she "split" him with her sword, "ground" him with a hand mill, and "sowed" him in the fields. The result is the return of Baal and of weather and fertility. Michael Coogan points out that in this mysterious association of death and the agricultural process we have a metaphor for the mystery of weather and for the mystery of agriculture itself, the mystery by which the dead seed is transformed into a living plant (Coogan, *Stories*, 83–84).

After Anat defeats Mot, El has a dream of Baal's return and the restoration of fertility. He sends the sun to find the lost god, who returns and reasserts his power. In seven years, however, the struggle between death and Baal resumes, just as in nature, fertility and abundance are always under the threat of drought and devastation.

The Hebrew Creation and Flood

The creation myth of the Jews, also accepted by Christians and in great part by Muslims, is contained in the first two chapters of Bere'shit ("in the beginning," or Genesis), the first book of the Torah. The story is clearly written by two writers at different times, and there are significant conflicts between the two versions, especially in connection with the creation of humans. Genesis 1:1–2:3 is generally attributed to the so-called priestly tradition that emerged in the sixth century B.C.E. during or following the Babylonian exile. The creator is referred to as Elohim, the plural form including, presumably, all the Middle Eastern gods or *els*. Furthermore, there is evident influence of the Babylonian *Enuma Elish* in the vision of what might be called the early geography of the Hebrew creation story. There is also apparent Egyptian influence in the idea of Elohim speaking the world into existence (Beltz, 35).

In Genesis 1 we learn that Elohim created the earth and the heavens, that darkness "covered" the primeval waters. As in so many creation stories, further creation required the separation of the original components of existence, so Elohim created light, separated light from darkness, and named night and day. In the next few of the seven first days Elohim continued the separating or differentiating process by creating sky, seas, dry land, plants, stars, sun, moon, animals, and finally humans. In this version of the creation story, the first male and female humans were created simultaneously *after* the creation of plants and animals and were given guardianship of the garden. The seventh day of creation was the day Elohim rested and so established the Sabbath.

Genesis 2:4–3:24 was composed under the Jerusalem monarchy probably in about 950 B.C.E. by the Yahwist author (J). Almost cer-

tainly based on an earlier oral account, this story is concerned primarily with the question of the creation of humans and depicts a very personal and jealous god, one echoed in other biblical references to
creation (e.g., Job 26, Jeremiah 10, and Isaiah 45).

In this version of creation Yahweh-Elohim created Adam ("man"
or "earthly being") out of the dust (*adamah*, "earth") of creation and
then breathed life into him. Next he planted a garden—a place in
which he strolled about like a true landowner—in Eden, somewhere
in the east, and he placed Adam there, encouraging him to eat anything but the fruit of a particular tree, which would bring death into
the world. To keep the man company, Yahweh created animals and
instructed Adam to name them. Adam did so but was still without a
proper companion, so Yahweh designed a being out of one of Adam's
ribs, and Adam called the new being woman. Adam and the woman
were content in their nakedness in the garden.

But the woman was tempted by the wily serpent—mythologically
speaking, a shape-changing trickster figure—to eat of the forbidden
tree. The fruit of the tree, he said, would bring godlike knowledge. The
woman ate some of the forbidden fruit and gave some to Adam, who
also ate, and suddenly the two became aware of their nakedness—that
is, of sexuality—and sewed fig leaves together to cover their genitals.
They then hid from Yahweh, who, of course, found them. When Yahweh learned of the disobedience he cursed the serpent, created enmity
between the woman and the serpent forever (fear of snakes), announced
that women would suffer in childbirth, and made men the rulers of
women. As for men, they would have to work hard to stay alive. Men
and women would eventually suffer death—return to the earth (dust).
Finally, Adam and the woman were expelled from the garden paradise,
and the jealous creator placed angel guards around the tree of life so
that humans might not eat its fruit and become immortal like him.

Before leaving the garden Adam named the woman Eve (Hava,
"mother of the living"). Walter Beltz points out that Hava was a name
of a Canaanite snake goddess whose companion, as was often the case
with the early fertility goddesses, was a serpent, a phallic figure whose
name in Aramaic was Hevya (Beltz, 66).

What the Genesis 2 and 3 account does is to deprive the female
once and for all of her original and positive pagan status and to estab-

lish a sense of sin in connection with sexuality and the life cycle itself. Christians would make use of the story as the basis for the doctrine of original sin that would color that religion's mythology, its strongly patriarchal treatment of women, and its negative view of sexuality. Christians took this position in spite of the fact that original sin is not central to the teachings of Jesus but is, in fact, negated by his role in Christian myth and theology as the "new Adam," the death-defeating fruit available to all on the new tree of life, the cross.

The Hebrews, like so many ancient peoples, included in their mythology of the early period of human existence, the story of a deluge, a flood by which the high god cleansed a sinful world. The flood of Genesis 6 owes much to the flood story in the Sumerian-Babylonian story of Gilgamesh, in which the flood hero—the Noah figure—is Ziusudra-Utnapishtim. In the Hebrew account, Yahweh became disgusted with humankind and decided, in effect, to begin again with the process of creating living things. Noah, a good man, was told to build a boat (the ark) for his immediate family and representatives of the plants and animals so as to ride out a devastating flood. When forty days had passed—the forty days that prefigure for Christians Jesus in the wilderness—the passengers were able to leave the ark and to start over with a new life.

After the flood, God hung a rainbow in the sky as a symbol of a new covenant with humankind. In the Babylonian story the reconciling rainbow symbol was Inanna-Ishtar's necklace, which she flung into the sky.

Of particular importance to Hebrew mythology, in addition to Noah's understanding with Yahweh, was the story that among the surviving family of the patriarch were his sons Ham, the ancestor of the Egyptians and Canaanites; Japheth, the ancestor of the Greeks and Philistines; and most important, Shem, the source of the Semitic Babylonians, Assyrians, Arabs, and Israelites.

The Christian Creation

Although the early Christians, given their Jewish roots, incorporated the Genesis creation into their mythology, they were also strongly influenced by Greek philosophy. This fact is evident in the prologue to the Gospel of John (1:1–18), the fourth book of the New Testament, echoing the Stoics and especially the ideas of the first-century Jewish philosopher Philo Judaeas, who drew upon the Greek concept of Logos in place of the old concept of Sophia (divine wisdom) to express the first act of creation. For Philo and the Greeks, beginning with Heraclitus in the sixth century B.C.E., Logos was the ordering force of the universe—divine wisdom or reason, the power that turned chaos into cosmos in the beginning.

John identifies Jesus with the Logos or Word, indicating the presence of Jesus with God and *as* God from the beginning of time, thus asserting his preeminence among all prophets. Genesis begins with the words "In the beginning God created the heavens and the earth." John "clarifies" this understanding with the words "In the beginning the Word [Logos] already was." And he continues, "The Word was in God's presence, and what God was, the Word was. He was with God at the beginning, and through him all things came to be; without him no created thing came into being." And later, "So the Word became flesh"; that is, was born into the world as Jesus so that the world could, in effect, be created anew through the "flood-death" that was Jesus's sacrifice, a death symbolized by the sacrament of baptism, in which the initiate "dies" in the flood of the font and is "born again" into a new creation.

The Gnostic Creation

Generally speaking, the Gnostics were Egyptians, Essene Jews, and early Christians, "heretics" who practiced mystery cults based on the idea of "knowing" the divine. *Gnosis* is now preferred to the term *Gnosticism*—a religion of its own—as a label for this loosely connected group. An important figure for Gnosis was Hermes Trismegistos, identified with the Egyptian god Thoth, to whom is accredited the crucial saying "He who knows himself, knows the All" (Quispel, 556). Many of the Christian followers of Gnosis were particularly devoted to what might seem to some to be the mysticism of John's Gospel and to his definition of "eternal life: to *know* you, the only true God, and Jesus Christ whom you have sent" (John 17:3; italics added).

The Gnostic form of the Logos was sometimes the female figure of divine wisdom, Sophia. One Gnostic creation myth says that

Sophia, the spirit of wisdom, signified by the dove that also was the sign of the Holy Spirit, was the child of the primeval silence and that Sophia herself was the mother of both Christ and a female spirit called Achamoth. Achamoth produced the material world and gave birth to Ildabaoth, the son of darkness, as well as to spirits that were emanations of Jehovah (Yahweh). These spirits produced the angels and humans and, as Jehovah, forbade humans from eating the fruit of the tree of knowledge. But Achamoth came to earth as the serpent Ophis and sought Christ's help in order to convince humans to disobey Jehovah by eating the forbidden fruit so as to gain knowledge—gnosis. Later Sophia sent Christ to earth as the dove to enter the human man Jesus as he was being baptized by John the Baptist in the Jordan River (Walker, 951).

The Hero Myths

Danel and Aqhat

The Canaanite tale of King Danel and his son, the hero Aqhat, is contained in fragments of three Ugaritic tablets from Ras Shamra. As the tale opens, Danel is performing a seven-day ritual in hopes of being granted a son and heir. His patron god, Baal, hears his prayers and intercedes for him with the high god, El. El agrees that Danel shall have a son, and after appropriate ministrations by childbirth and marriage goddesses, Danel's wife conceives. In time the boy, Aqhat, is born. Aqhat's conception and birth, therefore, have something of the miraculous or at least the extraordinary that is present at the beginning of so many hero myths, including, for instance, those of Isaac, Moses, Jesus, Sargon, and Theseus.

When Aqhat has become a young man, the craftsman of the gods, Kothar, pays a visit and presents Danel with a magical set of bow and arrows, which Danel presents to his own son. The magical weapons are, again, reminiscent of other hero myths. Achilles receives a magic shield from Hephaistos; Arthur retrieves the mysterious Excalibur.

The impetuous love and war goddess Anat wants the weapons for herself and attempts to bribe Aqhat with precious objects and eventually with immortality. In keeping with the heroic formula of patriarchal cultures, Aqhat refuses the bribes and does so rudely, questioning the goddess's hunting prowess and by extension the ability of women in general to perform masculine deeds. Gilgamesh had insulted Inanna-Ishtar in a similar manner, and several Indo-European heroes—including, for instance, the Irish Cúchulainn—act out the formula with angry goddesses. The result of the insult is usually disastrous. It leads to the hero's death and/or to the barrenness of the land. In the case of Aqhat both catastrophes occur. There is perhaps the implication of sexuality in Anat's bribes, as there is in the similar situations in the Gilgamesh and Cuchulainn myths. This is especially so given her role as a love goddess and her connection to fertility.

Reluctantly, El agrees to his daughter Anat's demand of revenge. The goddess sends her follower Yatpan in the form of a bird to accomplish her wishes, and Aqhat is bludgeoned to death as he is eating. Immediately the land dries up, and soon Danel learns of his son's murder. Finding bits of Aqhat's body in the guts of the vultures that had been hovering ominously over his house, Danel buries them and begins a seven-year period of mourning—a metaphor for a seven-year drought.

It is left to the brave Pugat, Danel's daughter, an Ugaritic Elektra, to avenge her brother's murder. She decorates her body with rouge and a beautiful robe and makes her way to Yatpan's camp with a concealed dagger. There she seduces her enemy into a state of drunkenness, during which he boasts of killing Aqhat. Although part of the tablet is missing, we can assume that she achieves her goal of revenge, much as, ironically, Anat had avenged the death of *her* brother, Baal.

Michael Coogan finds a "coincidence of themes" here. The deaths of Baal and Aqhat, as well as of Osiris in Egypt, represent "threats to fertility." It is possible that as Anat dismembered Baal's killer, death (Mot), Pugat might well have dismembered Yatpan. In the context of Middle Eastern fertility myths, as in the Osiris myth, dismemberment often has to do with the scattering of the dismembered body as seed. Coogan believes that the Aqhat story continued, in the tradition of so many hero myths, with the hero's "restoration to life and the consequent return of fertility to the fields" (Coogan, *Stories,* 27–31; see also Gibson, 23–27).

Kirta

King Kirta (Keret), a good man, whose story is told in fragments on three Ugaritic tablets, has lost his wife and is without children. Like Aqhat, he performs a ritual hoping for divine intervention, and his patron—possibly his father—El, comes to him in a dream. El tells Kirta that after sacrificing to him and to Baal he must go to war against Pabil, the king of Udm. After laying siege to the city for seven days he must refuse Pabil's offer of gifts but must demand the hand of the king's beautiful daughter Hurriya (Huray).

When Kirta wakes up he immediately follows the commands of the dream. On his way to Udm he stops at a shrine of the goddess Athirat-Elat (Asherah) and promises a gift to her if he succeeds in gaining the hand of Hurriya. It is at such shrines that Abraham, Isaac, and Jacob would create their holy places.

Everything happens as the dream had foretold. Pabil reluctantly surrenders Hurriya and, at Baal's suggestion, El blesses the marriage, saying that Hurriya will produce eight sons for Kirta and that the first one will be nursed by Athirat and Anat. El also predicts the birth of eight daughters. But Athirat wonders threateningly why Kirta has not yet fulfilled his promise made at her shrine.

Perhaps because he has neglected the pledge to Athirat, Kirta becomes deathly ill, and Hurriya holds a feast and asks that sacrifices be made for her husband. It seems evident that the king's last hours—even if he is, in fact, the son of El—have arrived. Ilihu (Elhu), a son of Kirta, makes a speech suggesting that his father accept death. A daughter of Kirta is sent for to mourn him. Already the king's sickness—like that of the Fisher King of the Grail story—has caused the land to go barren. On Mount Zephon, the Canaanite Olympus, Baal is leading a ceremony to bring fertility back to the earth. And just in time El decides to intervene by way of the healing goddess Shataqat. He instructs the goddess to touch the sick king on his head with her wand and to wash his body. After this is done, Kirta revives, eats food, and returns to his throne.

But his troubles are not over. Like droughts, the king's problems are cyclical. Another cycle seems about to begin as Kirta's son Yassib complains that his father has neglected his kingdom. The clear implication is that Yassib believes that he should replace his father as king. The story breaks off as Kirta curses his son. Coogan compares this aspect of the myth to the story of King David and his rebellious son Absalom (2 Samuel 15; Coogan, "Canaanite Religion," 54–55). Like the myth of Danel and Aqhat, this is clearly a myth about the sacred nature of kingship and about the close relationship between the king's welfare and fertility and that of his land (see Coogan, "Canaanite Religion," 52–57; Gibson, 19–23).

Abraham and His Family

Abraham (at first Abram; Ibrahim in Arabic) is the mythical hero and father of the so-called monotheistic or Abrahamic religions—Judaism, Christianity, and Islam. Genesis 11–50 is a combination of several versions of the story of Abraham and his immediate descendants, told by the Yahwist contributor, who was writing in Judah in about 950 B.C.E. under the early monarchy, the so-called Elohist author writing in about 850 B.C.E., and the writers of the priestly tradition of c. 550–400 B.C.E. The story takes us up to the myth of Moses and the Exodus.

A man called Terah, who had several sons, including Abram, was said to have decided to move from Ur, the ancient city in Mesopotamia, to Canaan. Terah was accompanied by his grandson Lot and by Abram and Abram's wife, Sarai, who was barren. The group traveled northeast and stopped in Harran, where Terah, now 205 years old, died. This was the mythological era, when gods still spoke with humans, and it was in Harran that Yahweh came to the seventy-five-year-old Abram and urged him to move on to Canaan, where "I shall make you into a great nation" (12:2). So Abram journeyed down to Shechem, where there was a sacred tree (probably sacred to the Canaanite goddess Asherah), at which point Abram built an altar to Yahweh. He did the same thing in Bethel as he moved south, following a tradition of building altars to his tribal god on sites sacred to others.

Famine caused the group to move to Egypt, but after some time they returned to Canaan with a great deal of wealth and livestock. As the land could not support the people of both Abram and Lot, Lot moved to the Jordan plain near Sodom. Yahweh again spoke to

Abram, giving him the land of Canaan, and Abram moved around in the land and eventually erected an altar to Yahweh in Hebron. After Abram had assisted an alliance of tribes in a successful war and accepted no booty, Yahweh once again appeared to him and promised that after four hundred years of oppression his descendants would possess all of the land of Canaan from the Nile to the Euphrates.

As Sarai was childless and knew that Abram required a son, she gave him her Egyptian slave girl, Hagar, as a concubine, and soon a son, Ishmael, was born. When Sarai, now jealous, mistreated Hagar, Yahweh promised the slave that her son would be "like the wild ass . . . at odds with all his kin" (16:12).

According to the priestly authors of Genesis, Yahweh came to Abram when the patriarch was ninety-nine years old and announced that Abram was now to be called Abraham, "father of many nations." Yahweh would be his and his descendants' god. This was a solemn covenant between Yahweh and his people, whose sign of having accepted the covenant would be circumcision, a sign of community and of exclusivity, as the uncircumcised would be "cut off from the kin of his father" (17:14). Both Abraham and Ishmael immediately had themselves circumcised.

Yahweh told Abraham that Sarai was now to be called Sarah ("princess") and that in spite of her old age she would give birth to a child, Isaac. As for Ishmael, he too would be fruitful and would father a great nation. Three men—presumably angels—appeared to Abraham and confirmed the fact that Sarah would soon give birth to a son.

For a while Abraham lived in Gerar, among the Philistines, and there Sarah gave birth to Isaac. Sarah demanded that Abraham expel Hagar and Ishmael from his entourage. This he did since Yahweh informed him that although Ishmael would be the father of a great nation, Isaac would be his true heir.

When Isaac was still a boy Yahweh tested Abraham's loyalty by demanding that he sacrifice his son to him. Abraham agreed, but at the last minute Yahweh provided a sheep as a substitute for the child.

Sarah died in Hebron at the age of 127. Abraham died there at the age of 175. He was buried by Isaac and Ishmael in a cave in Hebron bought previously from its Hittite owners.

In his miraculous birth and his near death by sacrifice in childhood, Isaac contains familiar characteristics of other mythic heroes.

He is literally the child of the covenant. Isaac married Rebekah, a distant relative of his father's from Mesopotamia, and Jacob and Esau were the result. Jacob was wily, able to trick the hairy Esau out of his birthright. Rebekah, who preferred Jacob, perpetuated Esau's loss of his birthright as the older of the two boys by tricking the now old and blind Isaac into giving Jacob the blessing of inheritance. Esau displeased his parents by marrying Judith and Bashemath, Hittite women. Jacob pleased them by following their suggestion that he go to Mesopotamia to the family's old homeland to find wives related to him. This approach signifies the post-exilic priestly tradition of marriage only within the exclusive community.

On his way to Mesopotamia, near a shrine between Beersheba and Harran, Jacob lay down to sleep, using a rock for a pillow, and had a vision of a ladder rising to heaven and of Yahweh reasserting the Abrahamic covenant. Yahweh had confirmed the covenant earlier to Isaac as well, at Beersheba, in honor of which Isaac had built an altar and dug a well (26:23–25). Jacob woke up, made a sacred pillar of his stone pillow, and named the place Bethel. In Mesopotamia he fell in love with Rachel, a woman related to his family, but was tricked into marrying her older sister Leah. He had many children with Leah, and later he also married Rachel, who, though apparently barren, miraculously gave birth finally to Joseph, who is thus marked as a hero. There were also children by two slave women.

After a long stay in service to his in-laws, Jacob and his wives returned to Canaan. On the way Jacob was approached by a man who wrestled with him (32:22–30). The man was apparently Yahweh himself—"I have seen God face-to-face," proclaimed Jacob—and the man blessed Jacob and changed his name to Israel (meaning "El rules"). Rachel gave birth to another son, Benjamin, on the road to Ephrathah (Bethlehem). Benjamin and the first eleven sons of Jacob were the progenitors of the twelve tribes of Israel. As for Isaac, he died near Hebron at the age of 180 and was buried there by Israel (Jacob) and Esau, the father of the Edomites (35:28–29).

Israel and his children settled in Canaan, but Joseph's brothers were jealous of him, as the obvious favorite of their father, and they stripped him of the beautiful robe he had been given by his father and threw him into a cistern. Some Midianites removed him from the well and sold him to Ishmaelites who took him to Egypt and sold him to Potiphar, the captain of the pharaoh's guard. But the enslaved Joseph found favor with the pharaoh and became a powerful man in Egypt. Years later Jacob and Joseph's brothers and their families came to Egypt looking for grain in a time of famine. Joseph revealed himself to them and the family was reconciled. The pharaoh gave them land in Goshen in his kingdom.

When Israel (Jacob) died he was taken, according to his instructions, to Canaan, where he was buried with his father and grandfather. When Joseph died, at age 110, he was embalmed and placed in a coffin Egyptian style, having given instructions that in time he should be moved to Canaan. With the death of Israel and Joseph, the story of the patriarchal tribal hero Abraham and his immediate family comes to an end, and the mythological stage is set for the story of the Exodus. The whole Abrahamic myth serves as a bridge between ancient times and the actual presence of the Hebrews in Canaan and as a mythological justification for the particular role of Israel and the Jews in history. It serves particularly as a justification for the belief in monotheism and for claims of exclusivity and land rights that by extension and mythical adjustment have been taken up at various times by Christians and Muslims as well. These myth-fed claims on the part of the Abrahamic religions are very much alive in the turmoil that characterizes the Middle East today.

Moses

The life of Moses contains elements—canonical and apocryphal—that mark him as a true mythic hero, and certainly he is Judaism's greatest hero. The canonical story is the one contained in the last four books of the Pentateuch: Shemot ("names"; Exodus), Vayiqra ("and he called"; Leviticus), Bemidbar ("in the wilderness"; Numbers), and Elleh Ha-Devarim ("these are the words"; Deuteronomy). As in the case of Genesis, it is a story told from at least three perspectives, reflecting the realities of three periods in Hebrew-Jewish history. For the Yahwist writer of the "golden age" of King David, Moses is a true hero and follower of the great and often harsh king of the universe, Yahweh. The somewhat later Elohist writer, perhaps using earlier oral sources, develops the mythological aspect of Moses's biography, including his unusual birth circumstances, but stresses his talents as a military and clan leader. The post-exilic priestly writers acknowledge Moses's leadership but elevate Aaron as a priestly hero and emphasize the events that serve to justify aspects of temple-based Jewish laws and traditions. The story outlined here, as in the Torah, is an amalgamation of these three perspectives.

In Exodus we step tentatively into history, or at least into a highly mythological rendering of what was probably an actual migration of Habiru or Semitic foreigners from Egypt to Canaan in the thirteenth century B.C.E. At the opening of Exodus the descendants of the family of the long-dead Jacob and Joseph were no longer popular with the Egyptians. In fact, the Hebrews, now enslaved workers, had become so numerous that the pharaoh ordered that all newborn Hebrew boys were to be thrown into the Nile to drown. One mother—of the Levite clan—placed her baby in a watertight reed basket and set him afloat in the river. The boy's sister Miriam watched as the basket was discovered by a daughter of the pharaoh, who immediately adopted the child. Miriam quickly fetched the baby's actual mother and presented her to the pharaoh's daughter as a wet nurse. The leaving of the baby in a basket on a river ties Moses to the unusual beginnings of several mythological or legendary heroes, including, for instance, Sargon of Akkad and Siegfried in Germany.

Again, as is often the case with heroes, we move directly to the stories of adulthood. Moses killed an Egyptian for mistreating two Hebrew slaves and was forced to flee for his life. He found his way to Midian, not far from Edom, the land founded by Esau, and there he married Zipporah, a daughter of a Midianite priest called Reuel (sometimes Jethro). Moses lived in Midian for forty years as a shepherd while the Hebrews continued to suffer in Egypt.

One day Moses climbed a mountain (Horeb or Sinai) and there, out of a burning bush, a voice spoke to him revealing himself as Yahweh, the "I Am," the god of "your fathers," Abraham, Isaac, and Jacob (Exodus 3:14–15). Yahweh then placed Moses clearly at the second stage of the traditional hero journey by calling him to action. Moses was to go to Egypt to lead his people out of bondage into Canaan. At first Moses doubted his qualifications for such a role and "refused the call," as so many would-be heroes do. Through various signs, including turning Moses's staff into a serpent, Yahweh demonstrated that he would use his power to support his prophet. So Moses returned to Egypt, accompanied, according to the priestly author, by his articulate and priestly brother Aaron, to assist in the fulfillment of the covenant made with Abraham and confirmed with Isaac and Israel-Jacob (6:2–8).

Thus begins the great heroic quest of Moses and the Hebrews for the "promised land." When the pharaoh refused to let the Hebrews go, Yahweh, through Moses, sent a series of plagues to Egypt, always sparing the Hebrews: the Nile was polluted, frogs were rained down, maggots and flies covered the land, the livestock all died, locusts ate the Egyptian crops. When the pharaoh still refused to free the Hebrews, Yahweh arranged a final plague. Each Hebrew family was to mark its doorpost with the blood of a slaughtered lamb and to eat a ceremonial meal while the angel of death passed over the marked houses and killed the oldest male child in each Egyptian house. After this establishment of what for Jews would become the feast of Passover, the pharaoh was finally convinced to let the Hebrews go.

With the next great mythic event, Yahweh confirmed his identification of the Hebrews as his chosen people. As Moses and his people followed Yahweh's pillar of cloud by day and pillar of fire by night the pharaoh changed his mind about letting them go and followed them with an army. When Moses came to the apparent barrier of the Sea of Reeds he raised his staff over it, and Yahweh caused a great wind to push aside the waters so the people could pass through. When the Egyptians pursued, the god allowed the waters to return, drowning the pharaoh's army.

A period in the wilderness followed, during which the people complained to Moses and Aaron of their plight, and Yahweh sent manna, sacred food, on which the Hebrews fed for forty years. Drink was provided when, as commanded by Yahweh, Moses used his staff to strike the rock at Horeb and water came from it.

Perhaps the most important mythic moment of the Exodus was God's gift to Moses of the Ten Commandments and the Book of the Covenant, the Torah, on Mount Sinai. The people agreed to the commandments and to other laws outlined by Yahweh, but when Moses returned to Mount Sinai for a time they began to complain. To placate them and give them something concrete to worship, Aaron made a golden calf. Moses returned and in his fury at this apostasy broke the stone tablets on which God's words were recorded. Later Yahweh provided new tablets, which were stored in the portable tabernacle called the Ark of the Covenant, the symbol of Yahweh himself, that led the Israelites into battle. The ark would become an important element in Jewish mythology. Its cult was officially recognized by David after his conquest of Jerusalem (for Jews the City of David on Mount Zion) in about 1000 B.C.E. The First Temple, that of Solomon in c. 950 B.C.E., housed the ark and became the principal national and religious center of the Israelites. The ark disappeared when the Babylonians destroyed the Temple in 587 B.C.E., and it was not in the Second Temple, completed in 516 B.C.E. The "lost ark" has spawned a mythology that is both a part of Jewish religious culture and general popular culture.

The absence of the ark is of particular significance for Jewish worship. It is probable that synagogues, containing Torah arks representing the lost Ark of the Covenant, were first founded in Babylon during the exile. When the required pilgrimage to the Temple in Jerusalem became impossible after the destruction of the Second Temple, synagogue worship could serve as a substitute not only in Babylon but everywhere else.

The story of Moses continues in the three biblical books that follow Exodus. We learn how the Hebrews rebelled against Moses and Yahweh, going so far as to indulge in Canaanite fertility rites and Baal worship. Even harsh punishment by Yahweh failed to completely end the rebellions (Numbers 11–25). Deuteronomy contains the last speeches of Moses to his people, elaborating on the commandments and warning of the consequences if the Hebrews fail to honor the covenant. Moses blessed the people and then went up to Mount Nebo in Moab, from which place Yahweh showed him the promised land. The leader of the Hebrews, 120 years old, then died and was buried somewhere in Moab. The last verses of Deuteronomy affirm that "there has never yet risen in Israel a prophet like Moses, whom the Lord knew face-to-face." These verses celebrate his "strong hand" and "awesome deeds" (34:10–12).

The Heroes of the Israelite Conquest

The heroes of the conquest are many, and with them we make tentative steps from myth into legend and then history. The first hero is Joshua, whose role as the leader of what in fact was a historical invasion is clearly mythical. As Joshua leads the Hebrews into Canaan, the Jordan River, faced by the Ark of the Covenant, parts (Joshua 3–4). Amidst the blowing of ram's horns and led by the ark, Joshua leads the attack on and conquest of Jericho. Then, in the tradition of holy war, the Canaanite people are killed as a sacrifice to Yahweh. After several more victories, Joshua presides over a covenant ceremony at Shechem, where he bids farewell to his people (23–24).

Two important heroines are Deborah, a visionary judge, and Jael, who succeeded in killing a Canaanite general single-handedly. Another hero is Gideon, who with only a small force defeated the Midianites, former friends and apparent Yahweh worshipers who had provided Moses with a wife. A popular favorite among Old Testament heroes is Samson, an ascetic or Nazirite around whose life many apocryphal tales of Herculean deeds were built. As a grown man he killed a thousand Philistines with a donkey's jawbone (Judges 15:15). But after being seduced, betrayed, and shorn of his great strength by the femme fatale Delilah (the femme fatale being a traditional enemy of the patriarchal hero in myth and literature), he was captured and blinded. Eventually regaining his strength he sacrificed his own life in causing a temple to crash down upon his Philistine captors (Judges 16, 28–30).

Many heroic legends surround the historical figure of King David. As a boy he defeated the gigantic Philistine warrior Goliath with a slingshot, and after various victories and setbacks was actually crowned king of Judah and later of a united Israel. Most important, he conquered the Jebusite city of Jebus (later Jerusalem), which had long been a Canaanite religious center. It was David whose armies finally defeated or expelled the Philistines and Canaanites and achieved the borders promised by Abraham's god (2 Samuel 2–20). It is said that through the prophet Nathan, Yahweh established a covenant with David; descendants of David would rule Israel forever (2 Samuel 7:2–16).

Other Biblical Heroes

According to the story, it was through the machinations of Bathsheba, the wife stolen by David from the Hittite Uriah, that Solomon,
Bathsheba's son, succeeded David as king. It was Solomon who solidified his position by murdering David's oldest surviving son and right-
ful heir, who built the First Temple to house the Ark of the Covenant
and who was given a special blessing of wisdom by Yahweh (1 Kings
1:1–2:25; 5:1–8:51). After Solomon's death a rebellion of the ten northern tribes developed and they formed a separate kingdom, Israel, in
the north. The Davidic dynasty, supported by the tribes of Judah and
Benjamin, formed the nation of Judah, with its capital in Jerusalem.

The third major part of the Hebrew Bible is the Writings (Kethu-
vim). Perhaps the most memorable story of heroism in this section is
contained in the Book of Ruth. The story goes that an Israelite and
his wife, Naomi, escaped a famine by moving to Moab. There the
couple's two sons married Moabite women, one of whom was Ruth.
When both her husband and sons died, Naomi, wishing to return to
Israel, suggested that her daughters-in-law remain in Moab and take
new husbands. Ruth, the epitome of loyalty, who loved and respected
Naomi, determined to accompany her to Israel. There, advised by
Naomi, she visited the elderly Boaz, who fell in love with her. In spite
of being advised by Boaz to find a younger man, Ruth proclaimed her
love for the old man and married him. Ruth later gave birth to Obed,
who became the father of Jesse and the grandfather of David.

Still other biblical heroes were the prophets, who reminded the Israelites of their misguided ways before, during, and after the Babylonian
exile. These include, among many others, Elisha, Isaiah, Jeremiah, and
Ezekiel. One such prophet, of mythical dimensions, was Daniel
(Danel), whom Yahweh protected even in the lion's den in Babylon
(Daniel 6:1–28). An important heroine was Judith, a widow who in the
extracanonical *Apocrypha* was said to have decapitated the Assyrian general Holofernes, saving Jerusalem and bringing riches to the Temple.

John the Baptist

Although the New Testament figure John the Baptist may have been
historical, his biography contains elements that are clearly mythologi-

cal. Like so many Old Testament heroes—Abram and Samuel, for
instance—he was conceived by an apparently barren mother. This extraordinary conception placed him in a special category and established his credentials as a hero in the minds of Christians. Christian
scripture claims that it was John's role to prepare the way for the Messiah, the king who, according to the Old Testament, would one day
come from Yahweh to restore the Davidic line and glory (Matthew 3;
Daniel 9:25–26). New Testament mythology nearly always exists to
fulfill prophecies contained in the Old Testament. The writer of the
Gospel of Matthew, therefore, introduces John the Baptist by quoting
the prophet Isaiah: "A voice cries in the wilderness, / 'Prepare the way
for the Lord; / clear a straight path for him,'" and when Jesus approaches him to be baptized, John cries out, "It is I who need to be
baptized by you" (Matthew 3:14). In John's Gospel, even more clearly,
he recognizes Jesus as the Messiah: "There is the Lamb of God," he
says (John 1:29–37).

Jesus

The biography of Jesus is contained in the four Gospels (the word
means "good news") attributed to Matthew, Mark, Luke, and John, in
the Acts of the Apostles, also by Luke, and in various noncanonical
texts such as the Gospel of Thomas and the Gospel of Philip. Mark
and Matthew were Jewish followers of Jesus, writing in the period between 70 and 90 C.E., Luke was a Gentile writing in about 90 C.E.,
and the identity of John, who wrote in about 100 C.E., possibly in
Ephesus, is unknown. Along with the works of followers such as Paul
of Tarsus (once Saul), these writings contain mythic elaborations of
the historical life of the man Jesus, about whom little more is known
than that he was an itinerant Jewish reformer with a significant following, who was crucified in the first century C.E. by the Romans. It is
the mythical or extraordinary events in Jesus's life that make him a
particularly complete example of the heroic monomyth and a symbolic figure around whom a major world religion was formed.

The mythic hero story traditionally begins with the hero's miraculous conception. Jesus's mother was Mary, a young woman of Nazareth
who was engaged to a carpenter named Joseph, a descendant of the

Davidic line. Before her marriage, Mary was visited by the angel
Gabriel, who announced that she would give birth to a child to be
named Jesus, to whom "the Lord God will give . . . the throne of his
ancestor David." After pointing out that she was a virgin and being
assured that she would become pregnant not by a man but by the
Holy Spirit, she humbly accepted her role, which was to be the
Christ-bearer, mother of the Messiah (Luke 1:26–38). The point being made was that it was through Jesus that the Davidic covenant
would be fulfilled.

An angel appeared to Joseph in a dream to explain to him his be-
trothed's pregnancy, and when the time came the events of the familiar mythic circumstances of the Nativity occurred in Bethlehem, the
city of Joseph's family, that is, of David, where Mary and Joseph had
gone to be counted in a census. The obscure setting of Jesus's birth, a
stable (Luke 2:1–21), and what came in Christian tradition to be its
winter solstice date are in keeping with the second stage of the archetypal savior hero's life. The symbolic significance has to do with
the idea of revelation and salvation emerging from darkness. Under
Roman rule the Jews were in such darkness. Out of that darkness the
Messiah would come. The importance of the new child is indicated
in the story by the worshipful visit of humble shepherds as well as
wise men (magi) from the East, Gentile astrologers who could recognize a king, indicating a "kingdom" that transcended Israel
(Matthew 2:7–12).

Typically, the potentially world-changing young hero is threatened
by an outside force that resists the threat to the status quo. The baby
Zoroaster was threatened by the prince of the land, Duransarum. The
infant Moses, with all the other Hebrew infants, was threatened by
the pharaoh. The Christ child, after his circumcision (Luke 2:21), was
sought by the civil authority, Herod, and (like Moses) was saved, even
as all of the male babies under two in Bethlehem were massacred on
orders of the king. Joseph had been warned of the catastrophe in a
dream, and he and Mary had taken the child in time to the ancient
refuge of Egypt. This was done, says Matthew, to fulfill Yahweh's de-
claration, "Out of Egypt I have called my Son" (Matthew 2:13–15).
For Christians, Jesus would come out of Egypt leading a new spiritual
exodus to a new kind of promised land.

Canonical texts tell us little of Jesus's childhood. Luke says that on first being taken to the Temple in Jerusalem the child was recognized by the holy man Simeon and the prophet Anna as the Messiah (Luke 2:22-38). Luke goes on to say that the child grew into a young man in Nazareth and that when his parents took him to the Temple at age twelve, he had amazingly learned conversations with the temple elders and chided his parents for being upset by his straying away from them "in my Father's house" (Luke 2:39-52). The apocryphal gospels fill some of the gap between Jesus's childhood and adulthood. The fourth-century C.E. Gospel of Thomas, for instance, depicted the boy as a tricksterlike shamanic figure who turned dead fish into living fish and who made clay sparrows and then turned them into real sparrows (see Leeming and Page, *God*, 93-94). Typically, the world hero is revealed or recognized in childhood by such events.

In the case of the canonical Jesus the first great divine sign came at his baptism by John the Baptist, when God, speaking from the heavens, recognized Jesus as his "beloved son," that is, the Messiah (Luke 3:21-22; Mark 1:9-11; Matthew 3:13-17). The baptism is the test by water, perhaps referring back to the miraculous parting of the Sea of Reeds. The forty-day period of temptation in the wilderness that followed the baptism is also a reference to the forty years spent by Moses and the Hebrews in the wilderness and the forty days of Noah's flood. Later, Jesus would achieve another important stage of mythological status when, like Moses, he climbed a mountain and was recognized there—and miraculously transfigured—by God. On the mountain he met and talked with and, in effect, took precedence over Elijah and Moses, as later in Islamic mythology Muhammad, on his Night Journey to the heavenly heights from Jerusalem, would meet and supersede Jesus and Moses (Matthew 17:1-8). Other mythical divine signs followed: the turning of water into wine, the feeding of thousands with tiny bits of food, the curing of incurable illnesses and disabilities, the raising of the dead (John 11:1-44).

But the primary purpose of Jesus as he is depicted in the myths of the New Testament is to demonstrate symbolically the teachings of his ministry, his revised understanding of the promised land, and the kingdom to be established by the Messiah. This revision will also involve an assimilation of and broadening of the old Middle Eastern myths of fertility. We move from mere physical fertility and growth to the fertility and growth which are spiritual. As far as Christian theology is concerned, the new covenant expressed by the teachings and the mythic life of Jesus is one that, like the much earlier covenant with Noah, as opposed to that with the later Hebrew patriarchs, extends to all humanity.

The central myth of Christianity is that of the death and resurrection. According to the Passion story, told with only slightly varying details by the four Gospel writers, Jesus came to a point in his teaching and curing ministry when he realized he must enter Jerusalem to face the final and most important events of his life.

Jesus arranged to enter the capital city riding on an ass. The street was strewn with a carpet of cloaks and branches (traditionally palms in the Christian church) to signify royalty, and Jesus's followers cried out in praise, "Hosanna [O save us] to the Son of David" (Matthew 21: 6–13). Immediately Jesus entered the Temple and assumed messianic authority, throwing out the money changers, symbols of what he saw as the corruption of the Covenant.

On the Feast of the Passover, Jesus had his disciples arrange for a meal in an upstairs room. There he blessed Passover bread and wine as his "body and blood," suggesting a new "Passover" ceremony (Matthew 26:17–29; Mark 14:12–25; Luke 22:7–22; John 13:1–30). The sacrifice of Jesus would "save" the keepers of the reformed covenant and lead to new life. It is this ceremony that is repeated in churches everywhere. Like the post-exilic Jew in the synagogue, the Christian need not make a pilgrimage to Jerusalem. Although Christianity's center is there, at Golgotha, the place of the crucifixion, Jesus is said to be present wherever and whenever the ceremony of the Last Supper is repeated. That ceremony is itself symbolic of the actual sacrifice that is the subject matter of the rest of the story.

The Gospel writers report that Jesus was betrayed by a disciple named Judas, tried for heresy, and convicted. His captors dressed him ironically in a purple robe and a crown of thorns and mocked him as "king of the Jews," and later he was crucified. The crucifixion is the Christian version of the old Jewish Day of Atonement (Yom Kippur). The sacrificed Jesus becomes both animals of the ceremony, the animal sacrificed to God and the scapegoat animal that leaves with the community's sins transferred to it. He is also the sacrificial Lamb of God foreshadowed by the substitution of an animal for the almost sacrificed Isaac in the Old Testament and by the Passover lamb.

For Christians, the crucial event of this myth is the resurrection itself. After his death, according to tradition, Jesus, like so many heroes before him, descended to the underworld. There he harrowed hell and symbolically redeemed Adam and Eve (fallen humanity), indicating that through him the ancient original sin and the death that followed it could be overcome. Most important, on the third day after his death Jesus left the tomb and conversed with his followers. And forty days later he ascended into heaven, accomplishing the return from the land of the dead and the apotheosis that mark hero myths as various as those of Herakles and Quetzalcoatl (Matthew 22:23–33; Mark 12:18–27, 16:6; Luke 20:27–40, 24:7, 24:15–49; John 11:1–44, 20:9).

10

◈

The Mythology of Arabia and the Muslims

Arabian Mythology

Pre-Islamic Arabia, before it was influenced through various conquests by Judaism, Christianity, and perhaps Zoroastrianism, was polytheistic in its religion. *Jinn* (spirits) were worshiped, and various tribal groups worshiped their own, often astral deities. Cult centers were marked by temples, and by holy stones (*baetyls*) representing these and other tribal deities. Also sacred trees could serve as cult centers. For instance, Muhammad's tribe, the Quraysh, worshiped a great tree called the Dhat Anwat on the road between Mecca and Medina. Given the nomadic nature of many of the tribes, objects—especially stones—in any given place could be invested temporarily with the sacred and used as a focus of worship (see Allouche, 364).

An ancient permanent sacred stone cult center for the tribes of the Hijaz (western Arabia, in present-day Saudi Arabia), the land of Muhammad's tribe, as well as for other Arabs, was the Kabah in Mecca, with its mysterious Black Stone. In pre-Islamic times the Kabah was a pilgrimage center and sanctuary surrounded by some 360 idols, but there are indications that some Meccans even before the time of Muhammad were moving toward a concept of a single divine power (*al-ilah*, "the god"), perhaps in part under the influence of the Jews and Christians with whom they had frequent contacts (see Rahman, "Islam," 303–4).

Islamic Mythology

Islam is dominated by the person of Muhammad. Muhammad's biography is historically fairly clear, and Islam depends less on mythology than do Judaism and Christianity. Mythological tales of the
Prophet did emerge from folklore, however, and two essential myths,
that is, extraordinary or supernatural events, do mark his canonical
life. These are the passing to him by Allah (*al-ilah*) of the Qur'an
(Koran), the holy book of Islam, making him literally God's messenger, and his Night Journey to the seventh heaven.

Of course, the concept of Allah, the god of Abraham worshiped
also by Christians and Jews, is central to Islam. An important Islamic
myth concerns the "House of Allah," the old Kabah of Mecca, taken
over by Muhammad and his followers as the focal point of Islamic
worship. The Kabah is represented by every mosque, as synagogues
everywhere represent the ancient Temple of Judaism and churches
represent the place of crucifixion for Christians. The Kabah is said to
have been originally built by Ibrahim (Abraham) and left under the
guardianship of his son Isma'il (Ishmael), the founder of the Arabs.
The Kabah remained for a time a holy place to Jews and Christians
and people of other religions, too. But when the Prophet took control
of Mecca he destroyed all of the idols that surrounded the sanctuary
and it became primarily a goal of the Islamic pilgrimage, the hajj, and
the focus of the spiritual hajj, which is the act of prayer.

The Pantheons

As noted above, at first under the influence of Judaism and Christianity and especially later due to the teachings of Muhammad, the Arabs
moved from a polytheistic mythology to what the outsider might call
a hero-based monotheistic one.

As in the case of the development of Judaism, there is an early
struggle before and during Muhammad's career between monolatry,
in which a high god presides as the most important god among many
others, including important goddesses, and monotheism, which saw
the high god as the only god.

The High God

Scholars suggest that for some time before Muhammad the Meccans, as noted above, had associated the term *al-ilah* with the supreme divinity behind the tribal gods of Arabia, gods such as Wadd, Suwa, Yaghuth, Ya'uq, and Nasr in southern Arabia, several of whom, according to the Qur'an (71:23), were worshiped in the days of Nuh (Noah). Some Meccans had perhaps even worshiped Allah as their high god (see, e.g., Armstrong, *History of God,* 135–41; Gardet, 27). Karen Armstrong points out that when Muhammad began his preaching, the Quraysh already believed in Allah and that many "believed him to be the God worshiped by the Jews and Christians" (141). These Meccans apparently believed that the Kabah had in the beginning been dedicated to this deity, in spite of the supreme presence there of the Nabatean warrior rain god Hubal, the tutelary deity of Mecca. In fact, Muhammad's first biographer, Muhammad ibn Ishaq, records the possibly apocryphal story of several Quraysh traveling north to discover the ancient pre-Jewish, pre-Christian religion of Ibrahim (Armstrong, *History of God,* 136–37). These men might be seen as John the Baptist to Muhammad's Jesus. Ibrahim was considered a prophet and the first Muslim, because in his willingness to sacrifice his own son he demonstrated *islam,* total obedience to God (Van Seters, "Abraham," 17).

Allah is identifiable as the god of Abraham and the creator god of Jews and Christians, but as he reveals himself to his messenger Muhammad—for Muslims the "seal of the prophets," the interpreter with the last word, as it were—he projects different emphases than those of the God of Moses or Jesus. Like the Judeo-Christian deity, he is above all unique: "It has been revealed to me that your god is one god" (Qur'an 41:6). But the Qur'an (2:267; 4:171) specifically rejects the kind of theology that involves a divine intermediary between God and humans (e.g., a divine Jesus or Son of God) or a God of more than one aspect (e.g., the Christian doctrine of the Trinity). Allah is less personal than in his Judeo-Christian aspect, a more mysterious power, who is nevertheless behind all aspects of the universe. He is knowable only through his creation, through the signs of nature, the metaphorical stories of the prophets, and especially through the Qur'an, his great gift to humankind. And though he is al-'Azim, "the inaccessible," he is al-Rahman, "the compassionate," "the merciful." For the Islamic mystics or Sufis, especially, he is al-Haqq, "the real," "the true," and al-Hayy, "the living"—in some sense the god within (see Gardet, 26–35).

Goddesses

Goddesses played an important role in pre-Islamic Arabian religion and mythology. Manat, Allat (al-Lat, "the Goddess"), and al-Uzza are all mentioned in the Qur'an (53:19–22). Manat was worshiped in Qudayd, near Mecca, and in northern Arabia. She was a goddess of rain, health, victory, and destiny and was particularly honored during the pre-Islamic pilgrimages to the Kabah. Allat was popular in Taif, also close to Mecca. There she was represented by a large flat stone and smaller precious stones kept in a wooden box. Called "mother of the gods" and "mother of the sun," she protected travelers. Al-Uzza was the primary goddess of the Quraysh. She seems to have been a love goddess whose worship took place in a sanctuary made up of three trees.

Together these goddesses were the *banat al-Lah,* "daughters of God," and were much revered by the Meccans at various stone shrines. When Muhammad forbade the worship of the *banat al-Lah* many of the first Muslims revolted. The historian Abu Jafar al-Tabari, in the tenth century, wrote that Muhammad was so upset by the split in his followers over the goddesses that he gave in and created some false or "satanic" verses, verses inspired by Satan, that allowed the *banat al-Lah* to be thought of as intercessors, like angels. Many Islamic scholars doubt that the incident of the satanic verses ever occurred, but according to al-Tabari, the angel Gabriel instructed Muhammad to do away with the lines and to replace them with a condemnation of the worship of these "empty names" (Armstrong, *History of God,* 147–48; Qur'an 16: 57–59; 22:52; 52:39; 53:19–26).

The Cosmic Myths

The Muslim Creation and Flood

Muhammad essentially accepted the Genesis version of creation, with some alterations. In the *hadith* of Islam, the collection of traditional sayings, acts, and stories of Muhammad, Allah says, "I was a hidden treasure; I wanted to be known. Hence, I created the world so that I might be known" (Armstrong, *History of God*, 150). In short, humans, through an experiencing of the natural signs of Allah's creation, the most important of which is the Qur'an, would know Allah.

The Qur'an does not present the creation in a single unit, the way it is presented in Genesis. Rather, the story comes in bits and pieces in various *suras* (chapters).

As in Genesis, Allah created the world himself (36:81; 43:9–87; 65:12). What was once a solid mass he tore apart, and he made living things from water (21:30; 24:45). As for the creation process itself, it is said to have taken six days (7:54; 10:3; 25:59; 32:4). Allah created the dark and the light, the heavens and the earth, the astral bodies (6:1; 7:54; 21:33; 39:5). He said, "Be," and it was (6:73). He created the beasts of burden and those that could be used for meat (6:142), animals and plants of all kinds (31:10–11). He created Adam in his image out of dust or clay and in later generations by a small seed (semen) and said, "Be," and he was (3:59; 6:2; 15:26; 16:4; 22:5; 32:7; 35:11; 40:67). He created woman (traditionally Haiwa, Eve) out of the same material (4:1; 39:6). He also created hell for evil spirits (jinns) and bad humans (7:179). Allah ordered the angels themselves to bow down to his human creation, and all did except for Iblis (from the Greek *diabolos*), who claimed to be better than humans because he had been created from fire rather than dust (7:11–12; 15:27; 17:61; 38:75–76). For his disobedience Iblis was banned from paradise (7:13–18) but with permission to tempt humans (15:36–37; 17:62–63) until doomsday, when he and his followers—that is, unbelievers, who are also *shaitans*—would be sent to hell (7:27; 26:95).

Allah made a garden—a paradise—for the man and his wife but ordered them not to eat from a particular tree (2:35). But the *shaitan* (Satan, Iblis, the father of all *shaitans*) convinced them that the fruit of the tree contained the power that made angels and gods (7:19–22; 20:120), and the couple ate the fruit. It is noteworthy that it was the couple, not the woman first and then the man, who committed this sin. After eating the fruit the man and the woman became conscious of their nakedness and sexual feelings and covered their genitals (7:27). Allah scolded them for listening to his enemy, and their life became hard (20:115–21). Later, as in Genesis, God sent a great flood,

during which the prophet Nuh (Noah) and his family, representing
believers, were saved in an ark (sura 11).

The Hero Myths

Ibrahim and Isma'il

Ibrahim is the Arabic name for the biblical Abraham. Traditionally
Ibrahim was thought to be the father of Islam in the sense that he
"knew" the true God—Allah, the God later revealed as such to
Muhammad—before there were Jews or Christians. The Qur'an and
Islamic tradition contain many myths of this *khalilu'llah* or "friend of
God." One story says that Ibrahim cut up a crow, a vulture, and a pea-
cock and then revived them simply by calling to them (Qur'an 2:262).
It is believed that Ibrahim threw stones at the devil at Mina, near
Mecca, where to this day pilgrims on the hajj commemorate the act
by throwing stones at a pillar of stone. Islamic tradition holds that
Hajar (Hagar) was the first wife of Ibrahim and the mother of his first
son Isma'il (Ishmael). Hajar and Isma'il were sent away by the jealous
second wife, Sarah, mother of Ibrahim's second son, Ishak (Isaac),
also a prophet (Qur'an 4:163; Knappert, *Encyclopedia*, 136, 151, 162–63).
While Hajar and Isma'il were wandering in the desert, the angel Jibril
(Gabriel) opened the well of Zamzam for them so that they could
survive. This well is in the place now called Mecca, and pilgrims still
drink from it. Pilgrims also run between two hills, representing Hajar's search for water. The story says that later Ibrahim, feeling guilty
about having expelled Hagar and Isma'il, found his wife and child at
the well and with Isma'il built the Kabah (Qur'an 2:124–40) according to Allah's specifications, as revealed by Jibril.

   In the Qur'an, it is Isma'il who would have been sacrificed by
Ibrahim had Allah not substituted a ram. When Ibrahim, his face
drenched in tears, pressed the knife against his willing son's throat it
would not penetrate the flesh. In fact, the knife spoke to the distraught
father, telling him that the Lord had forbidden it from cutting Isma'il
(Qur'an 37:102–7). Isma'il is the symbol of the perfect Muslim child,
one fully obedient to God. Not surprisingly, Muhammad was said to
be a descendant of Isma'il (Knappert, *Encyclopedia*, 161–62).

Musa

An important prophet for Muslims was Musa (Moses). It is recognized that God called Musa and that he revealed the Tawrat (Torah) to him (Qur'an, 19:52; 20:9–23; 27:7–12; 28:29–35; 79:15–16). The Quranic stories of Musa are essentially the same as those of Moses in the Bible.

Isa and Maryam

Isa (Jesus) was the penultimate prophet of Islam. He is believed to be *al-masih*, the Messiah, and *kalima-t-allah*, the Word of God, but not the Son of God (Qur'an 3:40, 4:169, 171). Capable of miracles, Isa was especially successful at curing the sick (Qur'an 3:49, 5:30). In some sense Isa was "raised up by God" (3:55), and many believe that he will come back (Knappert, *Encyclopedia*, 160).

Isa's birth was miraculous. Maryam (Mariam, Mary) for whom sura 19 of the Qur'an is named, was visited by the angel Jibril, who lifted her dress and blew on her body, making her pregnant with the breath—the Word—of God's spirit. Maryam gave birth to Isa next to a withered date palm and washed the child in a well placed there by Allah. The date palm tree suddenly flourished, and Jibril came back and advised Maryam not to make excuses for her mysterious pregnancy and birth-giving, but to allow the young prophet to speak for her. Miraculously, Isa, although a newborn baby, could speak and announced himself as a prophet, and people accepted his mother and him (Qur'an 3:45–46; 4:171; 19:16–27; 21:91; 23:50; 66:12; Knappert, *Encyclopedia*, 198).

Muhammad

The Islamic equivalent of Exodus, the story of the journey from lowliness to power of a people chosen of God is the story of Muhammad. Muhammad was the great hero of Islam, the Prophet, the Messenger of Allah, the perfect man (*insan al-kamil*), the founder of the *ummah*, the Muslim community. This was a community that was to transcend barriers of race and ethnicity. Islam was to become, like Christianity before it, a universal religion. The *ummah* would replace the older Arabic community ideal of the *muruwah*, which stressed utter and complete obedience to the clan chief and the validity of the blood feud (see Armstrong, *History of God*, 133–34). Muhammad replaced the loyalty of *muruwah* with the ideal of *islam*, total obedience to Allah. Not surprisingly, however, since both *muruwah* and *islam* stress the importance of the group over the individual, elements of the old *muruwah* way sometimes surfaces in Islam even today.

What concerns us in this book are not so much the historical events in Muhammad's life as the mythic or extraordinary ones that resonate beyond the world of fact.

In the *hadith* and in folklore Muhammad became much more than a discontented merchant of Mecca, much more than a religious reformer; he became the world hero to whom God spoke directly and who could break the barriers of space and time in a journey to God's heaven.

Of Muhammad's birth Thomas Carlyle wrote, "It was as of a birth from darkness into light, Arabia first became alive by means of it . . . a Hero-Prophet was sent down to them with a word they could believe" (Carlyle, 101). In keeping with the desire to make Muhammad a version of what Joseph Campbell would later call the "hero with a thousand faces," there are, of course, many apocryphal stories of Muhammad's birth and childhood in spite of canonical Islam's tendency to avoid such stories in connection with the Prophet. A sixteenth-century Turkish miniature depicts Abyssinians attacking the Kabah only to have their elephants refuse to move on the place of the future Prophet's birth. The same series of miniatures reveals a Muslim annunciation myth in which a host of angels in a dream announces to Amina that she will give birth to a prophet and instructing her to name the boy Muhammad (meaning "highly praised"). Still another miniature shows the angels protecting Amina from the sun during the birth, and another depicts the Prophet performing the first pre-prayer ablutions (see website, "Muhammad's Birth"). Given to a wet nurse, as was the tradition, it was said that the baby Muhammad had such a strong sense of justice that he would suck from only one breast, leaving the other for his wet nurse's son. It is also said that when Muhammad was three he was taken to a mountaintop by two men (angels) from the sky who split open his abdomen, took a black grain from it—some say it was the heart—washed it with melted snow, and filled it with light before restoring the child to wholeness. Then Muhammad was weighed, but with the child on one side of the scale and numerous men on the other, the scale still favored Muhammad. Then a wise man said that even if the whole *ummah* were placed on the scale, Muhammad would outweigh it (from Rodinson, *Mohammed*, 16–17). Such myths were clearly intended to establish the special quality of the Prophet.

Two canonical myths, however, are arguably the most important in Islam. These are the story of the receiving of the Qur'an, the greatest miracle of Islam, and the story of the Night Journey and Ascension (*al-isra'wa miraj*).

Revelation came to Muhammad when he was forty. For some years he had retreated for meditation to a cave (Ghar-i-Hira, "the cave of learning") on Mount Hira (Jabal-an-Nur, "mountain of light") during the fasting month of Ramadan. On the seventeenth day of Ramadan during his fifth such retreat, Muhammad had the first of what would be many such experiences over a twenty-two-year period, experiences reminiscent of the mountain revelations to Moses and the mountain transfiguration of Jesus.

On the seventeenth day of Ramadan, as Muhammad was sleeping, he was overpowered by the presence of divinity, apparently as represented by the angel Jibril (Qur'an 53:1–18). The angel recognized Muhammad as Allah's Messenger (*rasul*) through whom Allah's words would be revealed directly to humankind. The angel taught Muhammad the proper rituals of prayer and then commanded him to recite or "say" (*iqra*) the words of Allah. Like Moses and so many heroes, Muhammad at first refused the call, saying he was not a reciter, not a *kahin* (soothsayer). Then the angel squeezed him three times, taking away his breath until finally Muhammad agreed to recite, beginning the Qur'an (recitation) with the words "Recite in the name of thy sustainer, who has created—created man out of a germ-cell! Recite—for thy sustainer is the Most Bountiful, One who has taught [man] the use of the pen—taught him what he did not know" (Qur'an 96:1; Armstrong, *History of God*, 137). Shocked by his vision, Muhammad turned to his wife, Khadija, throwing himself in her lap. Khadija recognized him as a prophet and reassured him, for which reason she is much revered by Muslims. Over the next twenty-two years the Prophet would receive the Qur'an, the true miracle (*mu'jizah*) of Islam, bit by bit (Watt, "Muhammad," 143–44; Armstrong, *History of God,* 137–40).

The myth of the Night Journey and Ascension is referred to in the Qur'an (17:1), where Allah is praised for bringing his Prophet from the Sacred Mosque (Mecca) to the Farthest Mosque (usually interpreted as al-Aqsa in Jerusalem, but for some it might refer to Allah's heaven). In tradition the story has developed from what was perhaps the reporting of a dream to a fully developed myth with several versions. It usually begins with Muhammad's rising from sleep and going during the night to the Kabah to worship. There he fell asleep only to be awakened by Jibril and two other angels, who washed his heart with the waters of the ancient well Zamzam, thus instituting a ritual followed by Muslims and suggesting the idea of a heart cleansed of sin and idolatry. Then the winged mule or horse al-Buraq arrived and was told by Jibril to carry Muhammad on a journey. According to some, this animal possessed a human soul and had in ancient times carried Ibrahim to the Zamzam well to find Hajar and Isma'il. As Jan Knappert suggests, the fact that Muhammad was permitted to ride on Buraq signifies that he was, in fact, continuing the mission of Ibrahim (Knappert, *Encyclopedia,* 163). Eventually Muhammad came to Jerusalem, where he prayed at the temple-mosque of the Rock as the de facto imam in front of Ibrahim, Musa, and Isa (Abraham, Moses, and Jesus), who thus recognized his supremacy among them and, in effect trumped the events of the Transfiguration of Jesus in the New Testament. Presented with a glass of wine and a glass of milk, the Prophet chose the milk and was praised by Jibril for having chosen the "true religion." With Gabriel Muhammad made the steep and difficult climb up the ladder (*miraj*) through the seven heavens, each with its own prophet, learning aspects of the future Islam on the way and finally reaching the place of divinity, where according to some Muhammad saw Allah and according to others he saw not Allah himself but signs of Allah. Many traditions are associated with the Night Journey. Most involve a series of symbolic events and side trips. It is said by some that, guided by Jibril, Muhammad flew on Buraq to Medina, where he was told to perform the prayers (*salat*) at the place where Islam would be established, and that Buraq took Muhammad on to Mount Sinai, where Musa had spoken with God, and to the birthplace of Isa. In most versions Muhammad passed through a series of symbolic visions representing the ignorance and sinfulness of humanity as well as the serene place of the faithful. A somewhat amusing anecdote in one version of the Night Journey tells how Allah ordered Muslims to pray fifty times a day and that when Muhammad reported this to Musa he urged that Muhammad return to Allah to request a less demanding rule. This Muhammad did, and the number of daily praying times was reduced to five. Another version of this incident says that Allah's order was for five praying times a day and that the Prophet rejected Musa's suggestion that he petition for fewer. There is a *miraj* story that tells of Musa weeping upon his realization that Muhammad had usurped his place in God's favor and that one day Muhammad's followers would outnumber his (Watt, "Muhammad," 145–46; Armstrong, *History of God*, 217–18; Knappert, *Encyclopedia*, 163–66, 204–5; Bowering, 552–56).

The ascent is a common world hero sign. It marks the lives of such religious heroes as Jelaladin Rumi, St. Augustine, or the character of Dante in the *Divine Comedy* and can serve, as the *miraj* story does for many Islamic mystics (Sufis), as a mystical metaphor for the individual's as well as the given community's ascent to wholeness or enlightenment.

Epilogue

◈

After surveying Middle Eastern mythology it is difficult to avoid connections between mythology and events taking place in the Middle East today. These events are dominated by Israeli Jews and Arab Muslims, with significant Christian participation. Two realizations would strike any observer not directly committed to any one of these groups—a Tibetan Buddhist, for instance, or an Indian Hindu or Native American animist. First, various violent, clearly immoral, and illegal actions (if we take international law and United Nations resolutions seriously) occurring in the Middle East today are all too often justified by significant and influential combatants on the grounds of what can only be called myths. Israeli occupation of Palestinian land is justified by promises of land supposedly made by God to a Semitic tribesman several millennia ago. Suicide bombing by Palestinians is justified by words that the same God supposedly said to another Semitic tribesman several millennia later. Christian interference in the Middle East—historically the interference has been violent—is justified by a sense of spiritual ownership of a place where two millennia ago a Semitic man, supposedly the son of that same God, died and came back to life. The reigning mythologies of the Middle East, the mythologies of the Abrahamic Semites and their followers—the monotheists—have exerted a devastating influence on the events there for several thousand years, and this influence shows no sign of abating. This is so in spite of the fact that the actual teachings of the religions in question are diametrically opposed to the actions justified by the myths. The Ten Commandments preached by Moses, the peaceful "good news" preached by Jesus, and the equality and justice preached by Muhammad are all clearly in moral disagreement with the positions taken by so-called fundamentalist Jews, Christians, and Muslims in the world today and in the past. Fundamentalists see their way as the only way. They forget that myths—themselves in all likelihood *factually* untrue—*represent* truths that are spiritual and philosophical. Myths help to build and to identify functional communities; they are not historical events that can reasonably be used to justify acts of violence and dominance.

In the thirteenth century the great Islamic Sufi mystic Jelaladin Rumi wrote:

> Sometimes visible, sometimes not, sometimes devout Christians,
> sometimes staunchly Jewish. Until our inner love fits into everyone,
> all we can do is take daily these different shapes. (Rumi, 82–83)

For Rumi, religions and their myths, their particular ways, were merely temporary shelters in which to live. Middle Eastern history, like the history of the world in general, is a history that confuses these mere shelters for ultimate reality.

Bibliography

◈

Adams, Charles J. "*Qur'an*: The Text and Its History," *Encyclopedia of Religion* 12:156–176.

Albright, William F. *Yahweh and the Gods of Canaan*. Garden City, N.Y.: Doubleday, 1968.

Allen, J. P. Translations of Egyptian texts in W. W. Hallo, ed., *The Context of Scripture*, volume 1: *Canonical Compositions from the Biblical World*. Leiden, New York, and Cologne: Brill, 1997.

Allouche, Adel. "Arabian Religions," *Encyclopedia of Religion* 1:363–67.

Arberry, A. J. *The Koran Interpreted*. London: Oxford University Press, 1964.

Armstrong, Karen. *A History of God: The 4000–Year Quest of Judaism, Christianity, and Islam*. New York: Knopf, 1993.

———. *Islam: A Short History*. New York: Modern Library, 2000.

———. *Muhammad: A Biography of the Prophet*. San Francisco: Harper, 1992.

Asad, Muhammad, trans. *The Message of the Qur'an*. Gibraltar: 1980.

Baring, Anne, and Jules Cashford. *The Myth of the Goddess: Evolution of an Image*. London and New York: Penguin, 1993.

Beltz, Walter. *God and the Gods: Myths of the Bible*, trans. Peter Heinegg. Middlesex: Penguin, 1983.

Bently, Peter, ed. *The Dictionary of World Myth*. New York: Facts on File, 1995.

Black, Jeremy, and Anthony Green. *Gods, Demons and Symbols of Ancient Mesopotamia*. Austin: University of Texas Press, 2000.

Bornkamm, Gunther. *Jesus of Nazareth*. New York: Harper Collins, 1976.

Borowitz, Eugene B. "Judaism: An Overview," *Encyclopedia of Religion* 8: 127–49.

Bowering, Gerhard. "Mi'raj," *Encyclopedia of Religion* 9:552–56.

Bowker, John, ed. *The Oxford Dictionary of World Religions*. Oxford and New York: Oxford University Press, 1997.

Brandon, S.G.F. *Creation Legends of the Ancient Near East*. London: Hodder and Stoughton, 1963.

Bryce, T. *The Kingdom of Hittites*. Oxford: Clarendon Press, 1998.

Budge, E.A.W. *Egyptian Religion*. New York: Bell, 1959.

———. *The Gods of the Egyptians or Studies in Egyptian Mythology*. New York: Dover, 1969.

Campbell, Joseph. *The Hero with a Thousand Faces*, 2nd ed. Princeton: Princeton University Press, 1968.

———. *The Masks of God: Creative Mythology*. New York: Viking, 1968.

———. *The Masks of God: Occidental Mythology*. New York: Viking, 1964.

———. *The Masks of God: Oriental Mythology*. New York: Viking, 1962.

———. *The Masks of God: Primitive Mythology*. New York: Viking, 1969.

Carlyle, Thomas. *On Heroes, Hero Worship, and the Heroic in History*. Lincoln: University of Nebraska Press, 1966 [1841].

Clark, R. T. Rundle. *Myth and Symbol in Ancient Egypt*. London: Thames and Hudson, 1959.

Cohen, Mark R. "Judaism in the Middle East and North Africa to 1492," *Encyclopedia of Religion* 8: 148–57.

Cohn, N. *Noah's Flood: The Genesis Story in Western Thought*. New Haven and London: Yale University Press, 1996.

Coogan, Michael David. "Canaanite Religion: The Literature," *Encyclopedia of Religion* 3:45–58.

———. *The Oxford History of the Biblical World*. Oxford and New York: Oxford University Press, 1998.

———. *Stories from Ancient Canaan*. Louisville: Westminster Press, 1978.

Cooper, Alan M. "Canaanite Religion: An Overview," *Encyclopedia of Religion* 3:35–45.

Cross, F. M. *Canaanite Myth and Hebrew Epic: Essays in the History of the Religion of Israel*. Cambridge, Mass.: Harvard University Press, 1973.

Currid, J. D. *Ancient Egypt and the Old Testament*. Grand Rapids: Baker Books, 1997.

Dalley, Stephanie. *Myths from Mesopotamia*, rev. ed. The World's Classics Series. Oxford and New York: Oxford University Press, 2000.

Eliade, Mircea. *Patterns in Comparative Religion*, trans. Rosemary Sheed. Cleveland and New York: Meridian, 1963.

———, ed. *The Encyclopedia of Religion*, 16 vols. New York: Macmillan, 1987. (Individual essays listed by author as appearing in *Encyclopedia of Religion* with volume and page numbers.)

Faulkner, R. O. *The Ancient Egyptian Book of the Dead*, ed. C. Andrews. London: British Museum, 1985.

Frankfort, H. *Kingship and the Gods: A Study of Ancient Near Eastern Religion as the Integration of Society and Nature*. Chicago: University of Chicago Press, 1948.

Frazer, Sir James. *The New Golden Bough*, ed. Theodor Gaster. New York: Criterion Books, 1959.

Frymer-Kensky, Tikva. "*Enuma Elishh*," *Encyclopedia of Religion* 5:124–26.

———. *In the Wake of Goddesses: Women, Culture and the Biblical Transformation of Pagan Myths*. New York: Free Press, 1992.

Fulco, William J. "Anat," *Encyclopedia of Religion* 1:262–63.

———. "El," *Encyclopedia of Religion* 5:73–74.

Fuller, Reginald H. "God: God in the New Testament," *Encyclopedia of Religion* 6:8–11.

Gardet, Louis. "God: God in Islam," *Encyclopedia of Religion* 6:26–35.

Gardner, John, and John Maier. *Gilgamesh: Translated from the Sin-Legiunninni Version*. New York: Knopf, 1984.

Gaster, Theodor. *Thespis: Ritual, Myth, and Drama in the Ancient Near East*. Garden City, N.Y.: Doubleday, 1961.

Gerber, Jane S. "Judaism: Judaism in the Middle East and North Africa Since 1492," *Encyclopedia of Religion* 8: 157–64.

Gibson, J.L.C. *Canaanite Myths and Legends*. Edinburgh: T. and T. Clark, 1978.

Gimbutas, Marija. *The Language of the Goddess*. San Francisco: Harper and Row, 1989.

Gurney, O. R. *The Hittites*. London and New York: Penguin, 1990.

Hallo, William W. *The Context of Scripture*, vol. 1: *Canonical Compositions from the Biblical World*. Leiden, New York, Cologne: Brill, 1997.

Hallo, William W., and William Kelly Simpson. *The Ancient Near East: A History*, Second Edition. Fort Worth: Harcourt Brace, 1998.

Harris, Stephen L. *Understanding the Bible*, 2nd ed. Palo Alto and London: Mayfield, 1985.

Hick, John, ed. *The Myth of God Incarnate*. London: Westminster John Knox Press, 1977.

Hinnels, J. R. *Persian Mythology.* London: Hamlyn, 1975.

Hoffner, Harry A., Jr. *Hittite Myths,* 2nd ed. Atlanta: Scholars Press, 1998.

———. "Hittite Religion," *Encyclopedia of Religion* 6:408–14.

Hooke, S. H. *Babylonian and Assyrian Religion.* New York: Hutchinson's University Library, 1953.

Jackson, Guida M. *Encyclopedia of Traditional Epics.* Santa Barbara: ABC-CLIO, 1994.

Jacobsen, Thorkild. "Mesopotamian Religions," *Encyclopedia of Religion* 9:447–469.

———. *The Treasures of Darkness: A History of Mesopotamian Religion.* New Haven and London: Yale University Press, 1976.

Kerrigan, Michael, Alan Lothian, and Piers Vitebsky. *Epics of Early Civilization: Myths of the Ancient Near East.* London: Duncan Baird, 1998.

Knappert, Jan. *The Encyclopedia of Middle Eastern Mythology and Religion.* Shaftesbury, Rockport, Brisbane: Element, 1993.

———. *Islamic Legends,* 2 vols. Leiden: Brill, 1985.

Kramer, Samuel Noah. *Sumerian Mythology,* rev. ed. New York: Harper and Row, 1961.

———, ed. *Mythologies of the Ancient World.* Garden City, N.Y.: Doubleday, 1961.

Kramer, Samuel Noah, and John Maier. *Myths of Enki: The Crafty God.* New York and Oxford: Oxford University Press, 1989.

Lambert, W. G. "A New Look at the Babylonian Background of Genesis," *Journal of Theological Studies* 16, 1965.

Leeming, David A. *A Dictionary of Asian Mythology.* New York: Oxford University Press, 2001.

———. *Myth: A Biography of Belief.* New York: Oxford University Press, 2002.

———. *Mythology: The Voyage of the Hero,* 3rd ed. New York: Oxford University Press, 1998.

———. *The World of Myth: An Anthology.* New York: Oxford University Press, 1990.

Leeming, David A., and Margaret Leeming. *A Dictionary of Creation Myths.* New York: Oxford University Press, 1995.

Leeming, David A., and Jake Page. *God: Myths of the Male Divine.* New York: Oxford University Press, 1996.

———. *Goddess: Myths of the Female Divine.* New York: Oxford University Press, 1994.

Leick, Gwendolen. *A Dictionary of Ancient Near Eastern Mythology.* London and New York: Routledge, 1991.

Lesko, Leonard. "Atum," *Encyclopedia of Religion* 1:519.

———. "Egyptian Religion: An Overview," *Encyclopedia of Religion* 5:37–54.

———. "Isis," *Encyclopedia of Religion* 7:302.

———. "Osiris," *Encyclopedia of Religion* 11:132–33.

———. "Ptah," *Encyclopedia of Religion* 12:81.

———. "Re," *Encyclopedia of Religion* 12:222–23.

———. "Seth," *Encyclopedia of Religion* 13:178.

———. "Thoth," *Encyclopedia of Religion* 14:493–94.

Macqueen, J. G. *The Hittites and Their Contemporaries in Asia Minor.* New York: Thames and Hudson, 1996.

Moran, William L. "Gilgamesh," *Encyclopedia of Religion* 5:557–560.

Nasr, Seyed Hossein. *Islamic Spirituality,* 2 vols. New York: Crossroads, 1987, 1991.

Nicholson, Ernest W. *God and His People.* New York: Oxford University Press, 1986.

O'Collins, Gerald. "Jesus," *Encyclopedia of Religion* 8:15–28.

Patai, Raphael. "The Goddess Asherah," *Journal of Cuneiform Studies* 24, 1965.

Pritchard, James B. *Ancient Near Eastern Texts Relating to the Old Testament,* 3rd ed. Princeton: Princeton University Press, 1969.

Quispel, Gilles. "Gnosticism: From Its Origins to the Middle Ages," *Encyclopedia of Religion* 5:566–74.

Rahman, Fazlur. "Islam," *Encyclopedia of Religion* 7:303–22.

———. *Islam.* Chicago: University of Chicago Press, 1979.

Rauf, M. A. *The Life and Teaching of the Prophet Muhammad.* London: Longman, 1964.

Redford, Donald B. "Egyptian Religion: The Literature," *Encyclopedia of Religion* 5:54–65.

Rodinson, Maxine. *The Arabs,* 2nd ed. Chicago: University of Chicago Press, 1981.

———. *Mohammed,* trans. Anne Carter. New York: Penguin, 1983.

Rumi. *Unseen Rain: Quatrains of Rumi,* trans. John Moyne and Coleman Barks. Putney, Vt.: Threshold Books, 1986.

Sandars, N. K., trans. *The Epic of Gilgamesh.* Harmondsworth: Penguin, 1973.

Sperling, S. David. "God: God in the Hebrew Scriptures," *Encyclopedia of Religion* 6:1–8.

Srejovich, Dragoslav. "Neolithic Religion," *Encyclopedia of Religion* 10: 352–60.

Stetkevych, Jaroslav. *Muhammad and the Golden Bough: Reconstructing Arabian Myth.* Bloomington and Indianapolis: Indiana University Press, 1996.

Suggs, M. Jack, Katherine Doob Sakenfeld, and James R. Mueller, eds. *The Oxford Study Bible.* New York: Oxford University Press, 1992.

Teixidor, Javier. "Aramean Religion," *Encyclopedia of Religion* 1:367–72.

Thomas. *The Gospel According to Thomas.* Leiden: Brill, 1959.

Van Seters, John. "Abraham," *Encyclopedia of Religion* 1:13–17.

Van Seters, John. "Moses," *Encyclopedia of Religion* 10:115–21.

Van Voss, M. Heerma. "Anubis," *Encyclopedia of Religion* 1:330–31.

Walker, Barbara G. *The Woman's Encyclopedia of Myths and Secrets.* San Francisco: Harper and Row, 1983.

Wasilewska, Ewa. *Creation Stories of the Middle East.* London and Philadelphia: Jessica Kingsley Publishers, 2000.

Watt, W. Montgomery. *Companion to the Qur'an.* London: Allen and Unwin, 1967.

Watt, W. Montgomery. "Muhammad," *Encyclopedia of Religion* 10:137–48.

Weinfeld, Moshe. "Israelite Religion," *Encyclopedia of Religion* 7:481–97.

Wolkstein, Diane, and Samuel Noah Kramer. *Inanna: Queen of Heaven and Earth.* New York: Harper and Row, 1983.

Index

139